RUDE FOOD

LUKE COX

SUMMERSDALE

Summersdale Publishers Ltd
46 West Street
Chichester
West Sussex
PO19 1RP
UK

www.summersdale.com

ISBN: 1 84024 277 9

Printed and bound by Cox & Wyman, Reading, Berkshire, UK

Front cover photograph © Chris Craymer/Getty Images

Contents

About this Book

If you want to cook to impress a loved one; or to turn a friend into a lover; or a stranger into a friend, then these recipes will only be as helpful as this advice: all you have to remember is that food, like life, should be about pleasure. If you keep that in mind while you cook, eat, chat and wash up (perhaps the next morning?), then I guarantee nothing can go wrong: you may burn the cheese sauce a little, or neglectfully over-fritz your scallops – but, really, who cares?

The aim of this book is to help you keep the pleasure and fun of cooking and eating on the metaphorical front burner. I've provided some ideas for romantic and clandestine meals that range from the teasingly erotic to the downright rude, and a dictionary of filthy food from which you can devise your own naughty nibbles and saucy snacks.

Most of the recipes in this book are for two, naturally, but sometimes, when more of an orgy is in order, the measures are for more. Feel free to reduce the quantities of ingredients to cater for whoever you happen to be entertaining ...

In researching this book I solicited the views of friends, peers, colleagues and random acquaintances (and my thanks to all those who responded to the Internet questionnaire). I asked: what sort of food turns you on? Which meals do you remember as being a little bit rude or saucy or romantic, and why? Although some responses revealed obscene perversions I've tried hard to blot from my memory (you know who you are), there was a common thread: it's not the food that makes the meal, it's the person you're with. So please make sure you eat while you have fun – and have fun while you eat.

What is Rude Food?

Food can be as rude as you want it to be, and in your teasing, tasting, licking and slurping experiments you've probably already discovered that the humblest of dishes can be the most unexpectedly erotic, while a crudely wrinkled turnip, genetically modified to resemble a giant phallus, may do nothing for you at all.

The fact is that what turns us on is as diverse as what makes us laugh, cry or want to kick someone, so whatever anyone tells you about the aphrodisiac properties of food, remember that experimentation is the key – and don't believe for a minute that just because you find eating cold baked beans an intensely spiritual and earth-shattering experience you are some sort of food pervert. Well, you are, but don't let it bother you. After all, it is only through eating a selection of bizarre and unlikely delicacies through the ages that we have arrived at our present understanding of what rude food actually is.

Throughout human history we have endeavoured to discover ways to improve our sexual prowess, to defrost the frigid and loosen our rigid inhibitions. As our lives, and especially our energetic sex lives, are dependent on food for survival, it isn't entirely surprising that these attempts have focused on what and how we eat.

The earliest principles of rude food worked on a simple premise: we *are* what we eat, so eating things that have huge, insatiable libidos will make us more like them – and if we eat things that are in some way deeply involved in the process of sex we'll be more like those things too. This led a bored Roman aristocracy to ingest huge quantities of genitalia in whatever form they could find them: monkey's testicles, boar's penises, and even deer vulva – no animal was safe from the rude food quest of this supposedly civilised people.

From this dark and unenlightened age of rude food experimentation a new philosophy evolved. Bored with centuries of chowing down boar cock with no discernible results, the Western world – in a flash of inspiration – decided this: it doesn't have to *be* the sex bit that you eat, it just has to *look* like it. Suddenly the hitherto undiscovered properties of a range of unlikely and otherwise unexciting foods were unleashed upon an unsuspecting public: oysters became the new black; melted butter was longingly teased from the drooping ends of asparagus spears; turnips and onions were looked at and handled in new ways they'd never before experienced, and which they rather enjoyed. These principles are still, in one way or another, with us today. We don't seriously believe that if something looks like a willy it will give us the raging horn, but if it works, roll with it. Hence you'll find this recipe book chock-full of suggestions involving artichokes (peel back the outer leaves to reveal the fruit within), saucily voluptuous avocado, prodigiously nipple-like strawberries, gently curving bananas, and so on and so forth.

All this, though, overlooks the most important principle of all rude food experimentation through the ages. It was largely an ignorance of the tenets of Eastern philosophy that condemned the ancient Roman civilisation to all those centuries of eating wholly unsavoury concoctions: while they were busy hacking off the private parts of whatever they'd caught that morning, the Buddhist, Hindu and Islamic quarters of the world were revelling in the discoveries they'd made about the internal effects food has on the brain and the body – and were having some pretty good sex while they were at it. They learnt all about pine nuts, and gingko, and coffee, and garlic, and ginger, and fennel, and honey, and chillies, and figs – and decided that while none of these things looked anything like their own body parts should look (well, perhaps the figs did, on a bad day), they were definitely doing *something*.

Today the question of whether there are any true natural aphrodisiacs is as clouded in folklore and myth as it was then, with scientists, the grumpy lot that they are, deciding they have better things to do than mess about with lobsters and truffles and placebos. We do know, however, that a healthy body equals a healthy mind, that a combination of both has a positive influence on our romantic and sexual ventures, and also that some foods contain vitamins and minerals that can help us with that extra touch of perkiness and zing just when we need it.

So, my disciple, I suspect you are no closer to knowing what rude food is than you were when you started reading. My advice is: journey through a world of saucy starters, irrepressibly frisky fish, incredibly naughty seafood and frankly cheeky desserts, and only then shall you find those first steps on the path to enlightenment towards the nirvana of the answer you desire. Or, failing that, cook up a few of the recipes, browse through the A-Z of rudeness at the back, and have a bit of fun in the kitchen while you do it. The world of rude food is now, officially, your oyster.

The Science Bit

If anyone tells you that cooking is a precise science they're either lying or spend all their time in the kitchen with their eyes glued to the pages of a cookery book, rarely looking up to fish out that tasty morsel lurking at the back of the fridge that would go oh-so-well with whatever it is they're knocking up out of Delia. I don't think there's a single recipe in the whole world that could be completely scuppered by an overly hearty application of your favourite herb, the grossly negligent omission of a cheese you consider ghastly, or the shock and unscripted inclusion of something random from the depths of your condiment drawer (the exception seeming to be cake-baking which, even if you follow the recipe precisely, seems to be a skill people only acquire with age). That said, one shouldn't ignore a recipe entirely, but instead use it as a handy guide, or a list of suggestions – in the spaces between the lines experiment away and, if you make an earth-shatteringly tasty discovery, *pretend it's what you intended all along*. It's a principle that works for me, anyway.

So assume the measurements in this book to be approximate and don't stress yourself out if you are a little over the recommended amount of monkfish and two ounces under on the potatoes – I have faith it will all come right in the end. Similarly, with the cooking times, different pieces of kit will cook at different speeds and you may, with experience, want to tinker about with the timing to make life easier for yourself. The preparation times quoted are based on my own chopping, peeling and coring speeds, which I hope you will find to be reassuringly unprofessional and pedestrian.

Oven temperatures are given in Celsius and Fahrenheit, but for those with plain old gas marks, here's a conversion table (all temperatures are approximate):

Degrees Fahrenheit	Degrees Celsius	Gas Mark
300	150	2
325	160-70	3
350	180	4
375	190	5
400	200	6
425	220	7
450	230	8

The technology you'll need to employ to be a rude food chef also shouldn't give you too much of a passion-killing headache. You'll find no recipes that require you to possess a 6-inch ramekin (does anyone have a ramekin?), and I'd like to think you'd find a way to cook most of these recipes if all you had access to was your granddad's wartime penknife and a fire. On occasion you'll need a food processor, even if it's one of those hand-held zizzer things (which are incredibly useful). Oh, and a syringe, which playfully pops up on page 120. I'd also advise investing in a nice pepper mill and salt cellar, as it's so much nicer to grind the stuff fresh. I've tried to avoid chef jargon at all times, but I will ask you to zest occasionally. This just means rubbing the skin of the citrus fruit over a cheese grater to get tiny slivers of the tangy peel.

Do remember that presentation means a lot to people. We eat and taste with our eyes, as much as we do with our mouths and noses. To get the most from your food invest in some attractive crockery, cutlery to match, and, of course, some candles, because everything in the world (and especially my cooking) looks better by candlelight.

Safe and Healthy Eating and Playing

There are worse betrayals you could offer a lover than food poisoning. However, nothing kills passion faster than stomach cramps, diarrhoea and a call to your GP, so for the sake of both your relationship and your health, stick to these simple DO'S and DON'TS when preparing, cooking, eating and playing with food.

DO wash your hands before preparing or cooking food.

DON'T allow raw meat, fish and seafood to come into contact with cooked food, vegetables, salads, etc. Use separate chopping boards and utensils for preparing raw meat, or wash them well between uses. DO wash your hands well if they've come into contact with raw meat BEFORE you handle any other implements or food.

DO thoroughly cook meat before it is served. For chicken, pork and reformed meats (i.e. sausages and burgers) this means the meat must be cooked through. Test chicken and pork with a skewer or knife to check no pink colour remains, and in the case of chicken that the juices run clear. With sausages and burgers I advise cooking an extra one which you can slice in half to check it is thoroughly cooked: a small financial penalty to pay for peace of mind. Steaks and other cuts of red meat should be cooked so that no pink colour remains on the outside.

DO wash vegetables before cooking and salad vegetables before serving – I'd do this even if you're buying packet vegetables that say they're ready-washed, just for peace of mind. A salad-spinner is therefore a great piece of kit well worth investing in. Similarly, DO thoroughly rinse fruit before you eat it or cook it.

DO buy the freshest food available, be it meat, fish, vegetables or dairy products. Freshness will always taste better, and in the case of fish, which in some instances can be served raw, is your guarantee of safety. DO try and buy free-range eggs – not only are you doing your bit for animal welfare, but they taste better too.

Rabelais famously wrote: 'The appetite grows by eating.' DO eat a healthy, balanced diet to ensure a healthy sexual appetite. Not just your sexual performance but your general wellbeing, weight, mental alertness and energy levels will be affected in the long term by the food you consume. DO eat a good balance of proteins, fats and carbohydrates, and avoid eating highly sugary foods too often. Also make sure you get plenty of fresh fruit and vegetables. DON'T be a crazy health freak – fat is not, in itself, bad for you: you need some as part of a balanced diet and avoiding it completely will be detrimental to your health.

For a more comprehensive guide to safe eating – especially if you find yourself storing and cooking large amounts of food – do invest in a copy of the latest edition of *Essential Food Hygiene*, published by the Royal Society of Health.

Now, that's the sensible bit out of the way: go out there and get cooking ...

Saucy Starters and Sexy Soups

Start your meals as you mean to continue them — have fun in the kitchen and at the table with light and tasty dishes you can share and enjoy. The key with starters is to keep them as simple as you can, as simplicity will keep your hands and mouths free to ... do other things. Here are a few suggestions for teasing plates that won't fill you up, created from the rudest foods in the marketplace, with some sexy soup recipes crammed full of aphrodisiac ingredients.

SimpleSexy Avocado Vinaigrette

Serves 2 (with dressing to spare)
Preparation time: 10 minutes
Cooking time: N/A

Potentially the simplest and most irresistible starter of all time. Avocados have always been revered for their delightfully voluptuous curves and renowned for their aphrodisiac qualities. Served with this French dressing — with a slightly spicy sexy sting — they are ready in a jiffy, leaving your hands free for other important tasks ...

2 ripe avocados
2 tablespoons white wine vinegar
4 tablespoons extra virgin olive oil
½ teaspoon Worcestershire sauce
½ teaspoon English mustard powder
½ teaspoon sugar
½ teaspoon salt
2 drops Tabasco sauce
¼ iceberg lettuce to garnish

Mix together the mustard powder, Worcestershire sauce, Tabasco, salt and sugar in a bowl. Gradually drizzle in the olive oil, beating the mixture with a fork as you add it to keep it smooth. When all the oil's been added, do the same with the vinegar, adding it slowly until the vinaigrette begins to thicken a little.

Halve and stone the avocados (opinion is divided as to what the best way to achieve this is. I would punt for slipping the avocado lengthways onto a sharp blade and rotating the avocado 360° with the blade always in contact with the stone. Rotate the halves in opposite directions and the fruit will fall in two. If your avocado is ripe enough, the stone will pop out with a satisfying schlurp under gentle pressure from a teaspoon).

Place the halves in bowls, stone side up, and fill the wells to brimming point with the vinaigrette dressing. Scatter a little finely chopped lettuce over the avocados and serve immediately.

Parsnip Fritters with Sweet Citrus Sauce

Serves 2
Preparation time: 10 minutes
Cooking time: 1 hour

Parsnips are indisputably phallic vegetables – long, cylindrical, slightly bulbous, gently wrinkled – but for all that they are not particularly exciting to look at. However, boiled, mashed, lightly fried in a little fat and drizzled with a sweet citrus sauce they come into their own. Variants of this simple and easy recipe have been kickstarting sexy meals for well over 100 years, so the humble (and more than slightly naughty) parsnip must be doing something right …

for the fritters
4 medium parsnips (or 2 particularly big ones)
1 large egg
2 tablespoons single cream
2 tablespoons white wine
freshly ground nutmeg (just a pinch)
2 oz / 50 g butter or 2 tablespoons cooking oil
salt and freshly ground black pepper

for the sauce
4 teaspoons caster sugar
2 oranges (one to juice and zest, one to garnish)

Traditional recipes for parsnip fritters encourage you to boil the parsnips with their skins on which should then, like potato jackets, come away whole. I'd suggest peeling the things beforehand to prevent unnecessary hot-handed hassle. In any case, wash (and peel) the parsnips and boil them in lightly salted water for 35-40 minutes. Drain well, then mash the parsnips together with the cream, wine, egg, seasoning and a tiny sprinkle of nutmeg (¼ teaspoon should do) until smooth and even. With lightly floured hands, shape the mash into 6 even-sized balls, and press each one down on a flat surface so the balls form thick, round patties.

Heat the butter or oil in a saucepan until just spitting, and fry the patties for 5 minutes each side or until a rich, golden brown. Drain them on kitchen towel. Meanwhile heat the orange juice, zest and sugar in a small saucepan, stirring until the juice is simmering and the sugar has dissolved.

Arrange the fritters on a plate, interspersed with thin orange segments, drizzle the sauce over the top and serve whilst still hot.

Crostini alla Chiantigiana (Chicken Liver Pâté on Toast)

Serves 2-4
Preparation time: 15 minutes
Cooking time: 25 minutes (plus 2 hours to cool)

We all know what a fearsome reputation liver has for providing stamina and oomph when oomph is lacking. This erotic and satisfying recipe is derived from a traditional appetiser served in restaurants throughout the Umbria and Tuscany regions of Italy, is easy to prepare at home, and is the perfect start to any romantic meal.

8 oz / 225 g chicken livers
1 celery stalk, finely chopped
1 small carrot, peeled and finely chopped
1 small white onion, peeled and finely chopped
4 tablespoons olive oil
4 tablespoons dry white wine
2 oz / 50 g unsalted butter
1 garlic clove, peeled and crushed
salt and pepper to season
1 loaf good white bread (e.g., French stick or ciabatta)
salt and freshly ground black pepper

First get that fiddly chopping and peeling out of the way: peel and finely chop all the vegetables and chop the chicken livers. Next heat the oil and butter together in a heavy-based saucepan. When the butter has melted, add the chopped vegetables and the crushed garlic and sauté them over a medium heat for 10 minutes, stirring frequently. Add the liver pieces and continue cooking and stirring for 4-5 minutes, or until the liver has cooked through (no pink colour will remain).

Pour the wine into the pan and turn the heat up a little, simmering the wine down until it has almost all evaporated. Remove the saucepan from the heat, cover, and allow the contents to cool.

When cool, transfer the chicken mixture to a food processor, season generously, and purée until smooth. Put the pâté in a suitable container and refrigerate for a good couple of hours before serving. It can be served up straight away but the flavour seems to develop with time, and preparing ahead allows you less stress later on.

When ready to serve, heat the oven to 200°C / 400°F, line a baking sheet with foil and place chunkily sliced rounds of bread on it. Brush them with a little oil and bake them for 10 minutes or so until golden (or, if feeling lazy and distinctly uncontinental, bung the bread in a toaster). Spread the toast with generous lashings of pâté and serve to your ravenous, oomph-lacking guests.

Shrimp and Sesame Yin Yang

Serves 2
Preparation time: 10 minutes
Cooking time: 15 minutes

The juxtaposition of shrimp and sesame has long been used in Cantonese cooking to symbolise harmony within a relationship through the contrast between light and dark, Yin and Yang being the swirling opposites within a circle known better in the West as 'The 69 Position'. This dish, thought to be a potent aphrodisiac, is traditionally served at Cantonese weddings, and what goes on afterwards is anyone's guess ...

1 lb / 500 g fresh shrimp (or frozen, cooked if you must)
6 oz / 150 g baby / button mushrooms
3 tablespoons sesame seeds
3 tablespoons fresh parsley, chopped
2 tablespoons Chinese wine (or sherry)
2 tablespoons lemon juice
1 tablespoon sesame oil
1 tablespoon vegetable oil
1 spring onion, finely chopped to garnish

Heat the oils together in a saucepan (or a wok, if you want to look the part) over a medium-high heat. Cook the mushrooms briskly until slightly browned, and then add the sesame seeds and shrimp. Fry for 8-10 minutes, stirring well, then add the wine, lemon juice and parsley. Stir well, remove from the heat and serve hot in two small bowls, topping each with a smattering of chopped spring onion.

Pining Love Potion

Serves 2
Preparation time: 5 minutes
Cooking time: 10 minutes

Recent scientific studies to prove the reputedly potent aphrodisiac qualities of pine nuts had to be abandoned when the participants started jumping the placebo group and each other. I suggest you run your own rigorous and thorough testing programme and let me know how you get on ...

4 oz / 100 g pine nuts
3 egg yolks
½ pint / 300 ml hot chicken stock
½ pint / 300 ml double cream
1 teaspoon cayenne pepper

Whizz together the pine nuts, egg yolks and a drizzle of chicken stock in a food processor until it forms a smooth, even paste. Heat this mixture in a heavy-based saucepan over a gentle heat, adding the cayenne pepper and slowly stirring in the rest of the chicken stock and taking care not to allow the mixture to come to the boil. Finally, fold in the cream and serve warm.

   Delicious nibbled from the ends of breadsticks, carrot batons, sticky fingers, ankles and toes.

Prawn and Saffron Dipping, Scooping and Schlurping Paste

Serves 2
Preparation time: 5 minutes
Cooking time: 10 minutes

Saffron has a reputation for being crazily expensive – which, relative to other herbs and spices, it most definitely is – but weight for weight it works out cheaper than Sildenafil Citrate (Viagra® to you), has pretty much the same effect, tastes much nicer and gives dishes a pleasingly warm, red colour. Cooking with Viagra® turns out to be more than marginally less exciting ...

8 oz / 225 g prawns, cooked and peeled
2 large egg yolks
½ pint / 300 ml single or reduced fat cream
½ pint / 300 ml dry white wine
1 fish stock cube
0.5 g saffron
2 tablespoons fresh coriander, chopped

Whizz together half the prawns and the egg yolks, cream, wine with the fish stock cube in a food processor until smooth and even. Transfer the mixture to a heavy-based saucepan and heat gently, stirring constantly, until the mixture begins to thicken – taking care not to boil it.

Add the rest of the prawns to the pan, mix well to heat through, and serve with a handful of fresh, chopped coriander. Another great dish to get truly messy with – fingers a necessity, breadsticks optional.

Trout Breakfast and Nibbling Mousse

Serves 2
Preparation time: 15 minutes
Cooking time: 25 minutes

This mousse is delicately fishy, roundly warming and fluffy enough to lick and nibble from just about anything. Call me a food pervert if you like, but this one is best served in bed as a pre-breakfast treat, although it works well as a romantic starter to share.

1 lb / 500 g fresh trout, gutted
4 oz / 100 g potatoes (fluffy ones like King Edward or Desiree)
juice of 2 lemons
4 tablespoons cognac
1-2 oz / 25-50 g unsalted butter
2 ripe avocados (one for garnish)
1 teaspoon cayenne pepper
salt and fresh black pepper

Cook the trout by grilling it for 2-3 minutes on each side under a medium-high heat or, if feeling lazy, by microwaving it in a non-metallic dish for 4 minutes on high. Remove the head, tail and bones (this is marginally easier to do when cooked). Peel and boil the potatoes in lightly salted water until soft and mashable.

Melt the butter in a pan, and meanwhile whizz together the trout flesh, one avocado, lemon juice, cognac and potatoes in a food processor until smooth and fluffy. Add the butter, cayenne pepper and season generously with salt and pepper. Whizz in the processor again for 10-20 seconds.

Transfer the mousse to a bowl and let it cool in a refrigerator. Serve garnished with sliced avocado – a perfect dip for eating from hunks of crusty bread, fingers and lips.

Caviar Kisses

Serves 2
Preparation time: 15 minutes
Cooking time: N/A

It isn't true that wealth and power are the world's most potent aphrodisiacs, but you can put the theory to the test yourself by decadently indulging your lover with a spot of caviar and pretending you're Lord or Lady Muck, James Bond, or Dirk Diggler.

1 cucumber
¼ pint / 150 ml sour cream
2 oz / 50 g caviar (such as red salmon caviar)
1 tablespoon fresh dill, chopped (or 1 teaspoon dried dill)
1 tablespoon fresh chives, chopped
dill sprigs to garnish (optional)
freshly ground black pepper

In a bowl combine the sour cream, chives, dill and a twist of black pepper and mix well. Wash and trim the cucumber and slice it into rounds about ¼ inch / ½ cm thick. To assemble the kisses, simply spread each cucumber round with the sour cream and herb mixture, topping each slice with a small spoonful of caviar and a sprig of fresh dill. For an extra touch (to show you care), serve with hot buttered toast trimmed into heart shapes.

Rough Cut Guacamole

Serves 4
Preparation time: 15 minutes
Cooking time: N/A

Two Mexican classics next: guacamole, roughened with onion and with the gentle tang of coriander, is a messy feast of avocado goo and can make for an aphrodisiac dipping and sucking experience rivalled by no other, while chilli and basil combine with tomatoes to make a zinging wake-up call of a salsa.

3 ripe avocados
½ red onion, peeled and roughly chopped
1 small green chilli, deseeded and finely chopped
1 large garlic clove, crushed
1 dash Tabasco sauce
juice of 1 lime
2 tablespoons fresh coriander, washed and roughly chopped
½ teaspoon paprika

Halve the avocados, remove the stones and scoop the flesh out into a bowl. Mash the flesh with a fork and mix in the chilli, lime juice, garlic and Tabasco. Continue to mash until the mixture is smooth, then mix in the red onion. Stir well, cover and refrigerate for 1 hour.

Just before serving, stir in the coriander, garnish with a sprinkling of paprika, and serve with tortilla chips or vegetable batons to dip – or just lick it seductively from your partner's fingers.

Chilli and Basil Tomato Salsa

Serves 4
Preparation time: 15 minutes
Cooking time: N/A

The delicious combination of chilli and basil is a dangerous prospect for any nymphomaniac.

1 lb / 500g fresh, ripe plum tomatoes
1 small white onion, peeled and roughly chopped
2 large garlic cloves, peeled
2 tablespoons fresh basil (one big handful)
2 tablespoons extra virgin olive oil
1 drop Tabasco or pepper sauce
1 green chilli, deseeded and finely chopped
1 red chilli, deseeded and finely chopped
salt and freshly ground black pepper

Firstly dispense with the tomato skins: using a small sharp knife remove the hard nodules where the tomatoes were attached to the stalk, then immerse the tomatoes in freshly boiled water. After a minute or so remove the tomatoes with a slotted spoon and with a little pressure the skins should fall away. Whizz the garlic, onion and basil in a food processor in short bursts until finely minced. Halve the skinned tomatoes and add them to the mix: again, use short bursts so the salsa has a rough, coarse texture.

Turn the processor to its slowest setting and slowly drizzle in the olive oil until well blended, then add a tiny dash of Tabasco and a healthy whack of salt and pepper. Finally stir in the thinly sliced chillies.

The salsa can be served immediately, with the obligatory dipping delights of tortilla chips, but the flavour tends to develop a little if it is left covered and refrigerated for an hour or so beforehand.

Spinach, Apple and Coriander Soup

Serves 2
Preparation time: 20 minutes
Cooking time: 30 minutes

Warming, hearty and invigorating, this soup is packed full of goodness, is simple to prepare, and has superb mischief-making potential. Spinach contains fortifying vitamins and minerals, coriander and nutmeg are believed by many to be potent aphrodisiacs.

12 oz / 300 g spinach, washed and chopped
3 cooking apples (but any apples can be used)
2 oz / 50 g unsalted butter
salt and fresh black pepper
¼ teaspoon nutmeg
4 tablespoons fresh coriander, chopped
¼ pint / 150 ml single or double cream (optional)
juice of 1 lemon

Peel and core the apples, then chop them into small cubes. Melt the butter in a large saucepan over a low heat, add the apples and gently sauté them for 5 minutes, or until they start to brown and tenderise a little. Add the spinach, ¾ pint / 400 ml water and season generously, also adding a small pinch of nutmeg. (If you want a really smooth soup, allow the mixture to cool and then liquidise it before returning it to the pan.)Turn up the heat and bring the liquid to boiling point, then turn it back down, cover the saucepan and simmer the ingredients for 20 minutes. Just before serving, stir in the lemon juice.

Spoon out the soup into two suitable bowls and top each with a good fistful of chopped coriander and, if liked, a dollop of fresh cream.

French Onion Soup

Serves 2
Preparation time: 25 minutes
Cooking time: 1 hour

A bowl of perfect onion soup is a legal requirement for all visitors to France, and top scientists believe there may be a link between the purportedly potent aphrodisiac qualities possessed by onion and the notorious Gallic flair for lovemaking. But why should they have all the fun? Try this one out at home and see if the rumours are true …

1 lb / 500 g white onions, peeled and finely chopped
2 oz / 50 g unsalted butter
2 tablespoons plain flour
2 teaspoons salt
¼ pint / 150 ml brandy
1 pint / 600 ml beef stock
2 oz / 50 g Parmesan cheese, grated
2 oz / 50 g Gruyère cheese, grated
freshly ground black pepper
½ French stick
2 tablespoons extra virgin olive oil

In a large saucepan, and over a low heat, melt the butter. Add the onions and cook for 8-10 minutes, or until soft. Sift the flour into the saucepan, coating the onions, then add ¼ pt / 100 ml of the beef stock and continue to cook until the mixture thickens a little. When it has, add the salt, a twist or three of pepper, the brandy and the remainder of the stock. Turn up the heat and bring the liquid to a boil, then turn the heat back down, cover the saucepan and let it simmer away for 30 minutes, stirring occasionally. While it gently bubbles, heat the oven to 200°C / 400°F, slice the French stick into thin rounds and bake the slices in the oven for 10 minutes until crisp and dry.

To serve in the traditional (and impressive) manner, ladle the soup into bowls and cover it with a generous sprinkling of Gruyère cheese. Cover the Gruyère with two or three baked bread slices, gently drizzle olive oil over the bread, and top the bowl with the grated Parmesan. Place each bowl under a hot grill for 1 minute, and then serve immediately.

Speedy Asparagus Velouté

Serves 2
Preparation time: 10 minutes
Cooking time: 10 minutes

An incredibly quick and easy starter, which, as its name seems to suggest, is soft and velvety.

1 lb / 500 g asparagus tips
¼ pint / 150 ml single cream
¼ pint / 150 ml chicken stock
1 egg yolk
1 tablespoon chives, chopped
freshly ground black pepper

Trim and roughly chop the asparagus tips. Place them in a food processor and whizz until finely chopped. Add the cream, stock, egg yolk and ground pepper, replace the lid and continue to blend until smooth and even. Transfer the liquid to a saucepan and heat gently for 10 minutes, taking care not to bring the soup to the boil. Serve immediately, garnished with a sprinkle of black pepper and a handful of chopped chives on the top of each bowl.

Fennel, Liquorice and Shrimp Soup

Serves 2
Preparation time: 20 minutes
Cooking time: 20 minutes

Fennel and aniseed are supposedly two of the most potent aphrodisiacs known to humankind. Be warned - they work in such fearsome combination in this recipe that you might not make it to the main course ...

1 lb / 500 g fennel bulb
½ pint / 300 ml dry white wine
4 oz / 100 g cooked shrimps
1 chicken stock cube
¼ pint / 150 ml crème fraîche
2 tablespoons Pernod, ouzo or other liquorice aperitif
salt and freshly ground black pepper
handful of chopped coriander to garnish

Trim the fennel stalks down to the bulb, removing and discarding any wilted outer layer, and chop the bulb into small cubes. If you bought a bulb with fennel leaves – a rarity in supermarkets – reserve the leaves to use as a garnish later. In a heavy-based pan heat the white wine, ½ pint / 300 ml water and chicken stock together with the pieces of fennel until boiling. Boil for 5-7 minutes until it reduces a little, then transfer the mixture to a food processor and whizz it together until it forms a smooth purée.

Allow the mixture to cool, then return to the pan. Heat until simmering, but not boiling, then add the crème fraîche, Pernod and shrimps and mix together well, seasoning generously.

Serve hot with buttered toast and a sprinkling of fennel leaves to garnish – a smattering of fresh chopped coriander will serve just as well and will add a new, subtle flavour.

Sweet Potato and Basil Soup

Serves 4
Preparation time: 25 minutes
Cooking time: 30 minutes

I've never heard anyone say that sweet potatoes are rude, although in their knobbly, unorthodox way they do look a little bit funny. However, they are a delight to eat, be it mashed with a tiny bit of butter and pepper or boiled down to make a creamy yet cream-free soup. Basil, meanwhile, is the queen of herbs and has been famed for centuries throughout Asia for its aphrodisiac and invigorating properties. The combination works wonders for a hearty and cosy winter warmer.

4 large sweet potatoes
2 large onions, peeled and chopped
2 medium carrots, peeled and diced
1 large celery stalk, diced
6 tablespoons fresh basil (2 big handfuls of leaves)
2 bay leaves
½ teaspoon dried thyme
¾ pint / 200 ml semi-skimmed milk
1 vegetable stock cube
1 oz / 25 g unsalted butter
nutmeg (a tiny pinch)
salt and freshly ground black pepper
2 tablespoons single cream and basil sprigs to garnish

Melt the butter in a large, heavy-based saucepan over a low heat. Add the chopped onions, carrots and celery and gently sauté them until the onions begin to turn brown and gold. Peel and chop the sweet potatoes into cubes and add them to the saucepan along with the bay leaves, thyme and nutmeg, the crumbled stock cube and enough cold water to just cover the vegetables. Turn up the heat and bring the water to the boil. Cover the pan and allow the contents to simmer for 15-20 minutes or until both the carrots and sweet potatoes are tender and fall apart easily when tested with a fork.

Drain the solid ingredients in a colander – with a bowl underneath to catch the stock – and place them in a food processor with 4 tablespoons of the liquid. Whizz them together until you have a smooth and even purée. Return both the stock and purée to the original saucepan and stir them together well. Return to a low heat, gradually add the milk and season well. Simmer like this for 10 minutes, or until ready to serve. Wash, dry and chop the basil, then stir it into the soup 5 minutes before you serve up.

Serve in bowls with the crustiest, tastiest bread and, for an extra touch, a small swirl of single cream and a sprig of basil delicately balanced on top of the soup.

Summerly DeVito's Crostini ai Carciofi (Artichokes on Toast)

Serves 4
Preparation time: 10 minutes
Cooking time: 10 minutes

Summerly swears by this tasty Italian snack as a perfect romantic starter (also great on crackers), and we can finally reveal the secret of why crostini in Italy tastes so good (it's all in the garlic).

1 tin or jar of artichoke hearts
1 loaf ciabatta bread / good white bread
3 oz / 75 g Parmesan cheese
1 tablespoon mayonnaise
1 large garlic clove
salt and freshly ground black pepper

Empty the artichoke hearts into a saucepan with a little of the juice and heat them gently until they begin to soften. Add the Parmesan cheese and stir it in well, mushing the hearts with a fork to form a semi-mash. Heat through for 2 minutes, then remove from the hob.

Meanwhile, heat the grill and slice the ciabatta loaf into rounds 2 or 3 cm thick. Peel the garlic clove, bash it with the back of the knife, then rub the crushed clove all over the faces of the ciabatta slices. Grill them until they are golden.

When the artichoke mix has cooled a little, add the mayonnaise, a little salt and a big twist of pepper. Smear the mixture on the ciabatta slices and serve.

Frisky Fish

Fish is exceptionally rude for all the right reasons: it is light, tasty and wonderfully good for you as it is crammed full of the vital vitamins and minerals everyone needs. This makes it perfect for the main course in any rude food experience because it won't weigh you down or leave you bloated, while making you feel pure and innocent throughout – well, at least until dessert. The potential for showing off – when all you've really done is something incredibly simple – is also huge, as fish flesh is great both for gentle wafting flavours and strong, spicy overtones. Mix it up with raucously fruity aphrodisiac ingredients, fresh herbs and vegetables, and cheeky smatterings of bread and butter for a meal to remember.

Baked Chatham Trout

Serves 2
Preparation time: 5 minutes
Cooking time: 20 minutes

The light, nutty flavour of almonds is intensified by roasting them for a little while beforehand, and they complement the delicate and flaky texture of fish perfectly. If served with some simple steamed vegetables, maybe a dollop of creamy mash, and eaten by candlelight, this is a perfect dish for seduction and indulgence.

2 trout fillets
2 tablespoons flaked almonds
1 tablespoon olive oil
salt and freshly ground black pepper

Pre-heat the oven to 200°C / 400°F. Mix the almonds and olive oil in a bowl, and spread the mixture over a foil-lined baking tray. Place on the top shelf of the oven for 10 minutes, or until the almonds start to sizzle and turn brown. Remove the tray and scrape the almond flakes into a bowl. Lay the trout fillets, skin side down, on the baking tray and season lightly with salt and pepper. Smear the flesh with the roasted almonds and oil. Return the tray to the oven for 10 minutes – until the trout is delicate pink – and serve immediately.

Marinated Red Snapper with Cognac Tapenade

Serves 2
Preparation time: 10 minutes (plus an hour's marinating time)
Cooking time: 25 minutes

Forget the fancy name — marinated fish is the simplest thing ever. Rustle up a mixture of oil, vinegar or lemon juice and your favourite herbs, cover the fish with it and give it a while to gently infuse through the flesh. These saucy snappers (one of the best fish ever), for instance, are marinated in sharp citrus and basil to complement the warming piquancy of their garlicky, capery, cognacky topping.

for the fillets
4 red snapper fillets
4 tablespoons extra virgin olive oil
2 tablespoons fresh basil
juice and zest of 1 lime
salt and freshly ground pepper

for the tapenade
2 oz / 50 g black olives, pitted
2 tablespoons cognac or brandy
1 tablespoon capers
1 large garlic clove
zest of 1 orange
2 tablespoons extra virgin olive oil
2 tablespoons Parmesan cheese
salt and freshly ground black pepper

Prepare the snapper fillets by rinsing them, patting them dry and then placing them, flesh uppermost, in a shallow dish, seasoning well with salt and pepper. Wash the basil and finely chop it, then mix it with the lime zest and spread both evenly over the fish. Pour the lime juice and then the olive oil over the fillets, cover the dish and leave it to marinate in a fridge for at least an hour before cooking.

Make the tapenade by whizzing together the cognac, olives, rinsed capers, garlic, orange zest, olive oil and Parmesan cheese in a food processor until smooth, and season to taste with salt and pepper.

Heat a griddle pan (or a frying pan, with no oil needed) over a high heat, remove the snapper fillets from the marinade, and cook them for no more than 1½ minutes on each side, searing the outside of the fish. Remove the fish from the pan and lay them in a shallow baking dish. Top each fillet with a generous smear of tapenade; transfer the dish to the oven and bake for 20 minutes at 200°C / 400°F. Serve fresh from the oven with some light, tasty vegetables such as broccoli or French beans.

Galician Thyme-Baked Hake
(Merluza à la Gallega)

Serves 4
Preparation time: 25 minutes
Cooking time: 1 hour

Those Galicians have a reputation in the rest of Spain for always being up to no good — perhaps this is why: tasty, salty and light fish topping a chunk of invigoratingly infused carbohydrate. Try it and see — you'll never go back to shepherd's pie ...

1 lb / 500g hake fillets
6 oz / 150 g red onions, finely chopped
2 lb / 1 kg floury potatoes
1 tablespoon flour
1 large garlic clove
2 tablespoons fresh thyme, chopped
2 bay leaves
1 tablespoon fresh parsley, chopped
1 teaspoon paprika
2 oz / 50 g unsalted butter
2 tablespoons olive oil
1 teaspoon green peppercorns
salt
thyme sprigs to garnish

Rinse the hake fillets well under cold water then pat them dry with kitchen towel. Cut the fillets into thick slices and leave the slices refrigerated in a covered dish. Peel and chop the potatoes into thin rounds.

Heat the oil and butter in a large, heavy-based saucepan over a low heat, and gently fry the onions, stirring continuously, until they begin to turn a golden brown. Crush and add the garlic along with the parsley and paprika, then add the potato slices. Sift the flour into the saucepan and continue to heat, turning the temperature up a little and stirring continuously.

When the potato rounds begin to turn a little translucent and brown at the edges, add cold water to the saucepan until the water just covers the contents. Add a good pinch of salt, the peppercorns, bay leaves and chopped thyme. Bring the liquid to the boil then cover and allow it to simmer for 15 minutes.

After this stew has bubbled away for a quarter of an hour the potatoes should be tender. Using a slotted spoon, transfer all the solid contents to a large baking dish, spreading them evenly along its base, adding three tablespoons of any remaining liquid. Top the dish with the hake slices, pressing them gently into the potato mixture, sprinkle a pinch of salt and a further tablespoon of thyme over the fish, then place the dish in the oven for 10-15 minutes at 200°C / 400°F. Serve, garnished with a sprig or two of thyme, directly from the dish.

Orange and Fennel Seed Crusted Halibut

Serves 2
Preparation time: 20 minutes
Cooking time: 6 minutes

Fennel, with its dreamy hit of aniseed, has been revered as a potent aphrodisiac for centuries. Try fruitily crusting these fillets and find out if the rumours are true ...

2 halibut fillets, boned
zest of 2 oranges
2 teaspoons fennel seed, ground
2 eggs
2 tablespoons single cream
2 tablespoons olive oil
3 tablespoons fresh white breadcrumbs
salt and freshly ground black pepper

You will need two mixing bowls – in one mix the orange zest, fennel, breadcrumbs, a generous pinch of salt and a good twist of black pepper. In the other whisk together the eggs and cream. Immerse the halibut fillets in the egg and cream mixture, and then coat one side of the fillet with the breadcrumb, zest and fennel seed mixture.

Heat the oil in a frying pan over a medium heat. When hot, lay the halibut in the oil crust side down, and fry until the breadcrumb crust goes golden brown (after 2-3 minutes). Flip the fillets over and continue to fry for a further 2-3 minutes, or until the flesh is firm to the touch.

Irish Garlic Butter Monkfish Tail

Serves 2
Preparation time: 15 minutes
Cooking time: 30 minutes

This classic dish has helped the Irish seduce one another on starlit nights for years, and contains a whack of garlic – fearsomely renowned for its purifying and aphrodisiac qualities – to make your eyes smile, along with other bits of you.

1 lb / 500 g monkfish tail fillets
3 oz / 75 g unsalted butter, plus 1 oz / 25 g to grease dish
2 large garlic gloves
2 eggs
2 tablespoons single cream
1 tablespoon fresh thyme, chopped
1 tablespoon fresh marjoram, chopped
juice of 1 lemon
2 tablespoons fresh white breadcrumbs
4 tablespoons plain flour
salt and freshly ground black pepper

Leave the butter out overnight so it softens to room temperature (or soften the butter with short bursts in the microwave and mash it with a fork). Crush the garlic into a bowl, add the butter, marjoram and thyme, and mix the whole lot together well. Chill in the refrigerator until hard again.

While the oven heats to 200°C / 400°F, lay the monkfish tail fillets on a baking dish. With a sharp knife make a slit in each into which you can pack the garlic and herb butter, folding the slit up so the butter won't fall out. Beat the eggs and cream together in a bowl. In another bowl sift the flour and mix with a good pinch of salt and a generous twist of pepper, and in a third bowl place the breadcrumbs. Dip each fillet in the flour, then the egg and cream mix, then the breadcrumbs, pressing the breadcrumbs into the flesh. Melt a little butter and use some of it to moisten the inside of the baking dish, and then return the fillets to it. Drizzle the rest of the butter, then the lemon juice, over the top of the fillets.

Place the baking dish in the oven, cooking the fillets for 30 minutes. Serve immediately with crusty bread to mop up the bubbly buttery dribbles.

Dijon, Caper and Green Pepper Skate Wings in Beurre Noisette

Serves 2
Preparation time: 10 minutes
Cooking time: 10 minutes

Skate wings are up there with oysters, shark fin and lobster as a food likely to put you in the mood for love. It's not clear why this is – one theory has it that they are high in zinc, but scientific experiments to isolate their aphrodisiac component ended up with otherwise reserved men and women of knowledge rolling around on their notes after long sessions of dreamily staring into one another's eyes. I hope your own investigations will unearth that certain je ne sais quoi *the French swear by ...*

2 large skate wings
2 teaspoons capers
2 teaspoons green peppercorns
2 tablespoons Dijon mustard
2 oz / 50 g unsalted butter
salt and freshly ground black pepper

Melt the butter in a pan over a very gentle heat. Brush the skate wings with a thin, even coating of the butter, then with another thin, even coating of Dijon mustard, and a sprinkle of seasoning. Grill the skate wings for 2-3 minutes each side. While they are cooking, turn the heat underneath the rest of the butter slightly. It should begin to turn a golden brown with small particles of a darker brown colour – when it does, remove it from the heat so as not to burn it.

When the skate wings are cooked, arrange them on plates with a sprinkling of drained capers and green peppercorns. Carefully pour the butter over the wings using a wooden spoon to keep the darker brown pieces in the pan. Top marks go to the chef who serves this up with a simple spoonful of Buttery Mash (see page 105 for the recipe).

Lemon Sole Veronique

Serves 2
Preparation time: 10 minutes
Cooking time: 20 minutes

Sole Veronique is a classic French dish, usually served without adornment as a starter, or as a meal in itself. It is creamy and fulfilling, so I'd plump for the latter option. If it seems complicated at first glance, fret not — all one needs to do is poach the fish and reduce the liquid, adding at the end a healthy smattering of that decidedly rude fruit that is the grape.

4 lemon sole fillets (or Dover sole)
2 shallots, finely chopped
1 oz / 25 g unsalted butter
½ oz / 10 g plain flour
1/3 pint / 200 ml dry white wine
1/3 pint / 200 ml whipping cream
1 tablespoon fresh tarragon, chopped
juice of half a lemon
salt and freshly ground black pepper
generous handful of seedless, peeled green grapes to garnish

With this dish you'll save yourself some hassle by preparing the grapes and fillets a little in advance. For the fish, slice each fillet in two down the middle. Season each fillet-half lightly and then roll them up from the thin end to form tight little bundles with the skin side innermost. Next, remove the grape skins by immersing in freshly boiled water for 1 minute. The skins should simply pop off with a little pressure leaving the grape flesh intact. Put the skinned grapes to one side for use later on (the object of your desire will be mightily impressed that you peeled grapes for them).

When you're ready to cook, heat half the butter in a large

frying pan over a gentle heat, and add the shallots, frying them gently for 2-3 minutes. Remove the pan from the heat and arrange the fillet bundles within it, sprinkling them with freshly chopped tarragon and covering them with the white wine and lemon juice. Return the pan to the heat, turning it up to medium, and simmer the liquid. Cover the pan (with a plate if it doesn't have a lid,) and let the fish poach for 4 minutes.

As the fish cooks, warm a baking dish in the oven, and after 4 minutes remove the pan from the heat and the fillets from the pan (saving the poaching liquid), placing them in the warmed dish and covering them with foil so they retain their heat while you prepare the sauce. At the same time, turn on the grill, heating it up to a medium heat.

Gently melt the remaining butter in a small saucepan and mix in the flour with a whisk. Meanwhile, return the poaching liquid to the heat, bring it to the boil and allow it to reduce to a little over half its original volume. Stir in the cream and bring the liquid down to a simmer. Gradually add this liquid to the butter and flour mixture, whisking the whole time so the sauce stays smooth, and seasoning well. When it is all combined, pour it over the fillets in the baking dish and place the dish under the grill for 3 minutes, or until the surface of the liquid develops a light brown glaze. Serve immediately by spooning the fillets and sauce into two bowls, decorating each with a handful of skinned grapes.

Seductive Seafood and
Succulent Shellfish

Seafood has a naughty reputation that has become almost legendary. There can be few things more alluring than a plump, juicy prawn or a tender, delectable scallop, and as for oysters ... Like Casanova, you might swear by the feisty aphrodisiac zing they provide (and although I've never eaten fifty in the bath before lunchtime, I can testify that they work), but is this because visually they remind us of sexual organs, or because, as a nutritional analysis of the squishy little beasts would have us believe, they are packed full of zinc, a key mineral in testosterone and sexual lubricant production? I can't help feeling there is more to seafood's rudeness than sight and our bodies' chemical requirements would lead us to accept. I hope you'll find, like I have, that the naughtiness of seafood lies in the contact one must have with it in cooking and eating – the crushing, the cracking, the squeezing and slurping – and I hope you'll find it a pleasure to share and enjoy.

Sherry King Prawn Tapas

Serves 2
Preparation time: 10 minutes
Cooking time: 5 minutes

The Spanish know a thing or two about sherry, having invented the stuff, and it's used here in this classic tapas dish to give the biggest prawns you can find a sweet and lively zing. Delightful as a starter, perfect as a main with other small, shareable dishes, prawns are versatile, reliable, easy to prepare and incredibly tasty. I read somewhere that it is now known why prawns turn pink when cooked — I still say it's magic.

12 raw king tiger prawns
2 tablespoons olive oil
4 tablespoons sherry
Tabasco sauce
salt and freshly ground black pepper

Prepare the prawns by shelling them, then scoring the back of each with a small sharp knife and carefully removing the dark intestinal tract. Alternatively you could ask the fishmonger to do this for you, or buy ready-prepared prawns, but there's something immeasurably pleasing about doing this bit yourself.

Heat the oil in a frying pan or wok over a medium heat, add the prawns and fry for 3 minutes, or until entirely pink. Add the sherry and remove the pan from the heat. Throw in a couple of drops of Tabasco sauce, season well and serve in a dish for two to share.

You could just as easily make this dish with pre-cooked (pink) prawns — not as fun or as fresh, but still tasty. Simply cook for 1-2 minutes to heat the prawns through, otherwise use exactly the same method as above.

Belgian Beer and Bacon Mussels

Serves 4
Preparation time: 15 minutes
Cooking time: 10 minutes

As Obelix famously said: 'These Belgians are crazy!' Not content with foisting the humble sprout and mayonnaise with chips onto an unsuspecting world, they are also responsible for adding beer to just about every foodstuff imaginable. As a means of steaming mussels, though, they're on to a winner, and this recipe is warming, hearty and as tasty as a main course as it is as a starter.

12 oz / 300 g mussels
4 tablespoons lager
4 rashers smoked bacon (streaky or back), rind removed
2 tablespoons fresh thyme, chopped
2 tablespoons fresh basil, chopped
1 small white onion, chopped
1 large garlic clove, finely chopped or crushed
1 tablespoon olive or vegetable oil

Wash the mussels thoroughly, discarding any that are already open. Heat the oil in a large pan over a medium-high heat, and fry the onion, garlic and bacon for 5 minutes, or until golden. Add the mussels, lager, thyme and basil and cover the pan with a tightly fitting lid. After 5 minutes remove the lid and spoon the mussels out into serving bowls, discarding any that have failed to open.

Mussels look wonderful and seductive as they are, but a sprig of thyme as a garnish for each bowl wouldn't go amiss, and remember to provide an empty bowl for the shells.

Fruitily Dressed Spicy Scallop Salad

Serves 4
Preparation time: 25 minutes
Cooking time: 2-3 minutes

Whoever invented scallops? I'd like to shake them by the hand for their crazy creation — and maybe I'll get the chance one day. Part shellfish, part meat, all good, scallops are tender and gorgeous. Try frying them up oh so briefly in a little garlic for a super starter, or try something a little more adventurous. This salad is fruity, colourful and sexy as hell.

8 oz / 225 g scallops
1 large, ripe mango
1 small, ripe pineapple
1 red onion
1 red pepper
1 yellow pepper
1 small red chilli
juice of 1 lemon
1 tablespoon fresh parsley, chopped
1 tablespoon vegetable oil
1 oz / 25 g unsalted butter
4 large kale or lettuce leaves to serve

First do the chopping and dicing. Peel the pineapple, getting rid of all the remnants of spines, and cut the soft flesh away from the hard core. Slice the flesh into 1-cm cubes. Peel the onion, and slice it into thin strips; core the peppers and cut them into 1-cm hunks; and scrape all the seeds from the chilli and cut it into the finest strips possible. Finally peel the mango and cut the fibrous flesh away from the stone.

If necessary, prepare the scallops: in supermarkets, or from a fishmongers, they may be ready prepared, but if bought on the shell you will need to rinse them well, pat them dry and pull away the hard muscular tissue that faces the red coral.

To make the salad, heat the oil and butter in a wok or frying pan over a medium heat. Add the peppers, chilli and onion and fry for 1 minute. Turn the heat up a touch and add the scallops. Fry for a further minute, then stir in the pineapple and parsley and remove from the heat. Line a large dish with the kale or lettuce leaves and spoon the salad on top.

For the dressing, whizz together the mango flesh and lemon juice in a food processor until smooth. Spoon this mixture sparingly over the salad, and serve whilst still warm.

Stir-Fry Ginger Crab

Serves 2
Preparation time: 15 minutes
Cooking time: 5-6 minutes

Crab meat's forkably delicate fluffiness makes it a mouthwatering ingredient for any occasion, be it folded into mayonnaise for an exotic dip, or simply on its own with freshly melted butter for a main course of sheer simplicity and cracking good fun. Here it joins forces with fresh ginger, widely used in the East for centuries in tinctures and potions, now known worldwide as a classic stir-fry ingredient with a unique, invigorating flavour.

2 dressed crabs
4 large spring onions
4-cm piece of ginger, peeled
2 large cloves garlic
2 tablespoons oyster sauce
2 tablespoons sherry
good slug olive oil
1 tablespoon dark soy sauce
1 leek
1 small red chilli
1 tablespoon fresh coriander, finely chopped

Slice the leek into fine, 4-cm-long slivers and the spring onions into 2-cm-long slivers. Finely chop, mince or grate the ginger, peel and crush the garlic cloves, and remove the seeds from the chilli and slice it finely.

Heat the oil in a wok or heavy frying pan over a medium-high heat. Add the ginger, garlic, leek and spring onions and cook for 2 minutes, taking care not to brown or burn them. Add the crab meat (white and brown meat), the oyster sauce, soy sauce, the sherry and 1 tablespoon of cold water. Reduce the heat a touch and simmer the mixture for 3-4 minutes until it has reduced to a slightly thickened consistency.

If you have bought fresh crab, keep the shells, warm them under the hot tap, dry them well and serve the stir-fry using the shells as dishes. If not, serve on a bed of delicate, thin noodles (such as vermicelli), cooked according to packet instructions. Either way, serve topped with a sprinkle of freshly chopped coriander.

Provençal-Stuffed and Greek-Grilled Squid

Serves 2
Preparation time: 20 minutes
Cooking time: 30 minutes

Mint gives this squid the fresh sparkle of a Greek barbecue, while the herby stuffing is straight from the heart of Provence. The balance of these against the toothsome tenderness of squid makes for a delectably rude feast. Make sure you have plenty of cocktail sticks at the ready for this recipe ...

2 large prepared squid

for the stuffing
½ tablespoon capers, chopped
½ tablespoon black olives, chopped
4 spring onions, chopped
3 tomatoes
2 tablespoons fresh parsley
2 tablespoons fresh white breadcrumbs
1 large garlic clove
1 egg yolk
slug of olive oil
salt and freshly ground black pepper

for the mint oil
4 tablespoons olive oil
2 tablespoons fresh mint

It's best to make the stuffing first, but before you do, heat the oven to 150°C / 300°F. Prepare all the ingredients so you have them to hand: peel and crush or finely chop the garlic clove, roughly chop the spring onions, capers and black olives, and skin the tomatoes (by immersing them in freshly boiled water for a minute or so), removing and discarding the seeds and roughly chopping the flesh.

Heat 1 tablespoon of olive oil in a heavy-based saucepan over a medium heat and fry the spring onions, garlic and – if your squid came with them – squid tentacles, roughly chopped, for 2 minutes. Remove the pan from the heat and allow the mixture to cool.

Mix together the parsley, breadcrumbs and tomatoes, a generous whack of salt and pepper and, when cool, the onion mixture. Add the egg yolk and beat it all together well so it binds. Lay the squid on a baking tray and gently score the flesh diagonally with a sharp knife: this helps to keep the flesh from splitting but is mainly aesthetic, so there's no need to do it if the flesh seems particularly thin. Spoon the stuffing mixture into the squid body cavities, taking care not to overfill them: the flesh will expand slightly when cooking, so allow a little bit of room. Pin the ends of the squid with cocktail sticks so none of the stuffing can escape. Place the squid in the centre of the preheated oven for 20 minutes.

Make the mint oil by whizzing together olive oil and fresh mint in a food processor until you have a smooth, deliciously pungent liquid – this can be done at the time or as much as a couple of days in advance, but should be kept refrigerated. After 20 minutes in the oven, remove the squid and heat the grill to its highest setting. Brush the squid all over with the mint oil and grill 4 inches or so from the heat source for 4 minutes before turning, basting with more mint oil, and grilling for a further 4 minutes. When ready, the flesh should have puffed out a little and turned opaque, while the filling will be hot throughout. Serve simply, with a drizzle of any remaining mint oil and fresh, light, steamed vegetables.

Oysters on Ice

Serves 2
Preparation time: 10 minutes
Cooking time: N/A

I'm presuming you've heard the word about oysters, and that you don't need me to tell you they're rich in sea goodies like zinc – essential in testosterone and sperm production – that they have a reputation as the zingiest string in anyone's aphrodisiac bow, and that they look decidedly rude. So I won't. You get going and have a few au naturel: a perfect start to a rude food dinner.

12 fresh oysters
2 lemons
freshly ground black and white pepper
Tabasco sauce
24 ice cubes

It is traditional to eat oysters raw, so only buy them from a reputable market and keep them chilled as constantly as possible, eating them on the day of purchase. Open them just before serving for the freshest taste of the sea: this isn't terribly difficult once you get the knack.

First, scrub the oysters well to remove any grit. Wrap a tea towel round your left hand and hold the oyster firmly in it with the flatter side uppermost and the hinge towards you. Carefully work the sharp edge of a broad, heavy knife into the crack between the shells as close to the hinge as you can find purchase. Twist the knife until the gap pops open (you'll need to use a little force), then work the knife around the shell. The halves should then separate easily. Discard the flat shells, leaving the oysters themselves in the saucer-shaped shell. Check for and remove any small pieces of grit or shell, then loosen the oyster away from the shell with a small sharp knife.

Serve the oysters on a bed of crushed ice on a platter, interspersed with lemon segments.

How one should eat oysters properly is a matter for some debate, but you should provide Tabasco sauce and white and black pepper along with the lemon wedges. A squeeze of lemon, a dash of pepper and Tabasco, a forkful of oyster into the mouth, a sup of the juices from the shell with buttered brown bread to follow is most proper – but you'll probably find yourself knocking them back *sans* cutlery with a giggle and a grin.

Grilled Oysters Kilpatrick

Serves 2, or 4 as a starter
Preparation time: 15 minutes
Cooking time: 10 minutes

*Better known, peculiarly, as Angels on Horseback, a slice of
bacon with your oyster turns it into a respectable main course
for true oyster aficionados.*

12 fresh oysters
6 rashers bacon (streaky or back, but for best results use a
similar amount of pancetta, thickly sliced)
12 teaspoons Worcestershire sauce
6 teaspoons unsalted butter
freshly ground black pepper

Preheat the oven to 200°C / 400°F. Prepare the oysters,
separating the oyster from the shell as described in Oysters on
Ice. For each half-shell, top the oyster with half a teaspoon of
butter, a teaspoon of Worcestershire sauce, a smattering of
black pepper and half a rasher of bacon. Place the shells on a
baking tray and place them in the oven, near the top, for 8
minutes.

Meanwhile, heat the grill to a medium-high heat. Remove
the oysters from the oven and place them under the grill for 2
minutes, just to crisp up the bacon a little. Serve the oysters in
their shells.

Oyster Shooters

Serves 2
Preparation time: 15 minutes
Cooking time: N/A

So, oysters aren't quite your favourite. In fact, you've never tried them, and something about their squishiness scares you, but you've heard they'll turn you into Casanova and you're willing to try anything once. Put aside those irrational fears and knock back one of these. Be warned, though: oyster and vodka is so patently naughty that the Fish Restaurant Council Special Commission banned them from being served worldwide after protests from staff about all the mopping up and table legs buckling under the weight of frisky diners ...

2 oysters
2 teaspoons horseradish sauce
50 ml vodka

Prepare the oysters as you would for Oysters on Ice. Remove each oyster from its shell and place in a shot glass. Add a teaspoon of horseradish sauce and top to the brim with vodka, which, ideally, should be ice-cold. Down the hatch with 'em, all in one go, and let the naughtiness commence ...

Saffron Snails

Serves 2
Preparation time: 10 minutes
Cooking time: 12 minutes

Well, no one's ever sure quite what to do with these. They're not really meat, and they don't live in the sea, but snails seem to inhabit a weird crossover point between the two. Snails can be mildly fascinating to watch whilst alive. Dead and cooked, however, they usually engender either extreme disgust or gushes of superlatives. Global attitudes to food are so varied it almost seems bonkers to discriminate against the poor escargot for any reason other than financial as they are not dissimilar to some of the slimy beasts we regularly drag from the sea and devour – which is all a round about way of saying: give the slurpy, mushy snail a chance ...

24 shelled snails
2 tomatoes
1 red bell pepper
2 oz / 50 g celery
2 oz / 50 g unsalted butter
2 garlic cloves, peeled and crushed
0.2 g saffron
2 teaspoons fresh thyme, chopped
2 teaspoons fresh sage, coarsely chopped
salt

Skin the tomatoes (by immersing them in boiling water for a minute or so – then the skins should simply fall off with a little pressure) and de-seed the red pepper. Chop both into chunks and put them in a food processor with the celery. Whizz them together for 5 seconds so you have a vegetable mixture that is coarse and chunky, and while you're at it, preheat the oven to 200°C / 400°F.

Next, melt the butter over a low heat in a heavy-based saucepan. Add the crushed garlic, saffron, thyme, sage and salt, and cook the mixture for about two minutes, or until the aroma of the herbs begins to waft gently from the pan. Mix the coarse tomato, pepper and celery mixture into the pan, stir well, and remove from the heat.

Arrange the snails in the bottom of an ovenproof dish (you can buy special ramekins in which to cook snails – a Pyrex gratin dish will suffice), and cover them with the vegetable mixture. Place the dish, uncovered, in the middle of the preheated oven until the vegetables begin to brown slightly – this should take around ten minutes, but certainly leave the dish in for no longer than twelve, after which time the snails will begin to toughen. Serve immediately with Chablis or Chardonnay and sliced French bread.

Cheeky Chicken and Mischievous Meat

Chicken is undoubtedly the supple tart of the meat world – a pie into which every carnivore on the planet has dabbled their sticky paws at some point or another. This is not to demean her in any way: her versatility is her virtue, and every little part of the bird provides a different and unique pleasure. She is also tender, white and pure – like we were once, before we started on that headlong roll down the slippery slope, which began with a nibble on an apple and ended with us slurping sticky strawberry juice from our belly buttons.

Red meat can also be rude, as long as there's something brutal and bloody about it. When we eat red meat we like to forget that we should know better, and we like to pretend that, for a moment, the civilised sexuality of society is held in abeyance. However, be sparing: your rude food experience could be hampered by the medical condition technically known as Stodgy Belly. Keep your meat-eating light, your flavours fragrant, and your fun intense.

Spinach and Ricotta Stuffed Breasts

Serves 2
Preparation time: 10 minutes
Cooking time: 20 minutes

A crowd-pleaser, a saviour and a hero. There are few experiences as delightful as watching the creamy filling dribble seductively, bringing with it a gently crusted ribbon of green, from the hearts of these golden beauties. I think I'll have a nice sit down now. The technical bit is that spinach is an excellent source of fortifying iron, while nutmeg contains myristic acid, a chemical compound found also in the peyote cactus, that has purportedly incredible aphrodisiac effects.

2 chicken breasts
4 oz / 100 g washed spinach
4 oz / 100 g ricotta cheese
2 oz / 50 g Gruyère cheese
nutmeg
fresh black pepper

Preheat the oven to 200°C / 400°F. Bring a ¼ pan of water to the boil and steam the spinach over the boiling water for 2-3 minutes, or until it has wilted and reduced in volume a little. Remove it from the heat, drain well and gently squeeze out any excess water – a salad spinner is the best method.

As the spinach cools, take the two breasts, skinning them if needs be, and make a slit in each one with the sharpest knife you have. Slice through the middle, along the length of the breast, forming a pouch. Take care not to cut all the way through.

Next, place the spinach in a bowl and add the ricotta. Mix the two together well and add a sprinkling of black pepper and a generous grating of nutmeg (about ¼ teaspoon). Spoon the mixture into the breast slits, stuffing it in well and pulling the upper tiers of chicken forwards to reclose the pouches. Place the stuffed breasts in a baking dish, adding a slight smear or spray of oil to the underside of each, and place them in the centre of the oven.

Remove them after ten minutes, and grate the Gruyère over the top of the breasts. Return them to the oven for a further ten minutes, check that the meat is thoroughly cooked, and then serve as immediately hot and dribblingly spurting as you can keep them.

Strawberry Glazed Breasts

Serves 2
Preparation time: 15 minutes
Cooking time: 20 minutes

Strawberries have the power to make even the greyest men of politics momentarily exciting. They are a staple of food and sex games, second-rate porn films, and they are fearsomely nipple-like. You could have yourself a whole strawberry-themed feast – or simply combine their sweet juiciness with tender, plump chicken.

2 large chicken breasts
8 oz / 225 g strawberries
2 large spring onions, finely chopped
1 tablespoon fresh mint, finely chopped (or 1 teaspoon prepared mint sauce)
2 tablespoons white wine vinegar
2 tablespoons olive oil
juice and zest of 1 lemon
fresh black pepper

After putting aside a couple of strawberries to garnish the served chicken breasts later, purée the rest for about a minute in a food processor. If you want to get rid of the pips, mash them through a sieve with a fork. If you're feeling lazy, just do the food processor bit: the pips stay in, though I've never found a reason why this should be undesirable.

Mix the puréed strawberries in a bowl with the lemon juice and zest, vinegar, mint, a twist of pepper and the finely chopped onions, then whisk the olive oil in with a fork. Lay the chicken breasts in a baking tray and heap the mixture over the top. It's tastiest when prepared a few hours in advance, with the chicken refrigerated and marinating in the strawberry mixture for a good couple of hours before cooking.

To cook, preheat the oven to 200°C / 400°F, and place the baking tray in the centre for 12-15 minutes, removing the chicken every 4 minutes to baste with the strawberry mixture. As with all chicken dishes, check the meat with a sharp knife to see if the juices from the centre run clear before serving (which may be difficult with this colourful dish – if in doubt, err on the side of caution).

As a final touch, crisp the glaze a little by placing the breasts under a hot grill for about a minute. Garnish with the reserved strawberries, a dash of the remaining marinade, serve, smile, and look as sweet as you feel.

Pork, Beef and Garlic Albondigas

Serves 2-4
Preparation time: 10 minutes
Cooking time: 20 minutes

How could you not? Meatballs take pride of place on any tapas menu and are as rude to eat as they are to look at. Dispense with cutlery for garlicky, spicy, finger-licking and pleasantly spherical fun.

4 oz / 100 g spicy sausages
4 oz / 100 g lean beef mince
2 shallots, finely chopped
2 tablespoons fresh white breadcrumbs
2 tablespoons fresh parsley, chopped (and a little extra to garnish)
slug of olive oil
2 large garlic cloves
Tabasco sauce
1 large egg
salt and freshly ground black pepper

Slice the sausages along their lengths and remove the skins. Place the meat in a bowl and add the beef mince, shallots, breadcrumbs, parsley, egg, the skinned and crushed garlic cloves and plenty of seasoning. Mix the ingredients together well and with lightly floured hands shape the mixture into 13 even balls.

Heat the olive oil in a large frying pan over a medium heat. Add the meatballs (six at a time, depending on the size of your pan) and cook for 20 minutes, turning regularly and ensuring the balls are evenly browned. Slice a sample ball (hence you made 13 of them) through the centre to make sure it is cooked through before serving.

CHEEKY CHICKEN AND MISCHIEVOUS MEAT

Remove the balls with a slotted spoon and place them on a warmed plate, sprinkling them with a little finely chopped parsley as a garnish. Serve with cocktail sticks and plenty of Tabasco, or a similarly spicy sauce, in a separate dish for dipping.

Thai Turkey Love Balls

Serves 2-3
Preparation time: 40 minutes (inc. 20 minutes
to cool)
Cooking time: 20 minutes

The people of Thailand know a thing or two about aphrodisiac cooking – and it could be that the winning combination of fragrant lemongrass, fiery chilli and zinging ginger used in so many of their recipes is why we keep popping back to Thai restaurants on cold winter nights, looking for a little more than just fearsomely delicious food. Try this triumphant triumvirate of ingredients with your favourite vegetables, fish and meat – or, for an unexpected bonus, fashion them into naughtily globular balls.

12 oz / 300 g lean turkey mince
2 spring onions, finely chopped
1 stalk lemongrass, finely chopped
1 red chilli, deseeded and finely chopped
2-cm piece of fresh ginger, peeled and grated or minced
4 tablespoons fresh coriander
1 tablespoon cornflour
2 tablespoons fish sauce
1 oz / 25 g caster sugar
2 tablespoons vegetable oil
fresh black pepper

Heat together the sugar and fish sauce in a heavy-based pan over a low heat, stirring until all the sugar has dissolved. Remove from the heat and mix in the chilli, lemongrass and ginger. When cool, pour it into a mixing bowl with the turkey mince, spring onions, cornflour, coriander and a generous twist of black pepper. Mix well and then, with lightly floured hands, shape the mixture into even balls – you should get about 10 from this quantity of meat. Cover the balls and refrigerate them for at least 20 minutes (this will help them retain their shape when cooked).

To cook the balls, heat the oil in a frying pan over a medium heat. Add the meatballs and cook for approximately 15 minutes, turning every 2 or 3 minutes. Cut a sample ball in half to check it is thoroughly cooked, i.e., no pink colour remains.

Dry the balls on a plate covered in kitchen paper. These balls are at their most amorous served with a gentle sprinkling of chopped spring onions, fresh coriander and a bowl of sweet chilli dipping sauce.

Toad-in-the-Hole

Serves 2
Preparation time: 10 minutes
Cooking time: 40 minutes

The most peculiarly named of all British dishes, Toad-in-the-Hole dates back to 1782 when an Ilkley Moor farmer named McCavity caught 15 toads – that had been blighting his turnip crop – in a specially designed trap: a hole in the ground full of mouldy turnip offcuts. The villagers cooked him this feast in honour of his achievement, with the original 'hole' made from a mashed prize swede. Well, it's possible. Toad-in-the-Hole surely has to have a naughtier and more salacious origin, given its despicably rude connotations – but this recipe was taught to me by my mum, so don't tell her that …

6 best quality pork sausages
3 oz / 75 g plain flour
1 large egg
3 fl oz / 85 ml semi-skimmed milk
1 tablespoon cooking oil
salt and fresh black pepper

To make the batter, sieve the flour into a large mixing bowl and break an egg into the centre of the flour. Add a generous pinch of salt, a fair old whack of pepper and a dash of milk. With a wooden spoon blend these ingredients together, adding the rest of the milk little by little and stirring well, continuing the process with a whisk when the mixture is liquid enough. If there are any lumps, sieve the batter again to remove them. This mixture will also produce decent Yorkshire puddings (although if used for this purpose it should be allowed to stand for an hour – for Toad it doesn't really matter).

Next, preheat the oven to as hot as it will go (220°C / 425°F).

CHEEKY CHICKEN AND MISCHIEVOUS MEAT

Lightly fry the sausages in a little oil until they are evenly browned, then place them in a baking dish with a tablespoon of oil (or a little margarine), making sure the fat coats the dish evenly. Put the dish of sausages in the oven, and when the fat is properly spitting-and-bubbling hot pour in the batter. Quickly return the dish to the oven and cook on the highest heat for 20 minutes, or until the batter has risen. When it has, turn the oven down to a medium heat and cook for a further 20 minutes. After this time the sausages should be thoroughly cooked and the surrounding batter fluffy but crisp.

Best served with a side portion of veg and some nice, thick gravy.

Honey and Rosemary Roast Lamb (and Garlicky Roast Potatoes)

Serves 4
Preparation time: 15 minutes
Cooking time: 1–1½ hours

Lamb and rosemary have been passionate and acrobatic lovers in all their previous incarnations. Rosemary's hintingly naughty fragrance beautifully wafts through the meat while it cooks. That, and the warming gold of the sticky honey glaze, gives the humble leg of lamb a light and daring feel for the day, whisking you off to a hauntingly silent Mediterranean island for the evening.

for the lamb
½ leg of lamb
2 teaspoons English mustard powder
2 tablespoons clear runny honey
6 sprigs fresh rosemary, washed
salt and freshly ground black pepper

for the roast potatoes
1 lb / 500 g King Edward / white potatoes, peeled, washed and quartered
2 large garlic cloves
2 tablespoons vegetable oil

Heat the oven to 200°C / 400°F. While it heats up, mix a good twist of pepper and half a teaspoon of salt together with the mustard powder. Place the lamb in a roasting tin and rub this mixture all over it. Take a sharp knife and spear holes of about 2-cm depth all over the lamb. Chop the rosemary sprigs into short pieces of similar length and push them into the holes

76

you've just made. Cover the lamb with foil and place the roasting tin in the oven for 1 hour, removing it briefly after 30 minutes to remove the foil and baste with the juices, before replacing the foil and returning it to the oven.

After 1 hour, remove the foil, baste well, and drizzle honey over the lamb, ensuring an even-ish coating. Return the lamb to the oven for the remainder of the cooking time: the best way to calculate how long the lamb should take is to allow 20 minutes for each 1 lb / 500 g, plus an additional 30 minutes. So, a 1.5 kg (3 lb) cut will take approximately 1 hour 30 minutes.

If you find yourself twiddling your thumbs while the lamb cooks, entertain yourself by preparing some super garlicky roast potatoes. Parboil (boil until half-cooked) 1 lb / 500 g of peeled and quartered fluffy potatoes (like King Edwards) for 10 minutes in simmering salted water. Drain the potatoes and return them to the empty pan. Add 2 tablespoons of vegetable oil and 2 large crushed garlic cloves, then place a lid on the saucepan and vigorously bash the potatoes about inside to mash and fluff up the edges. Place them in a baking tray and add them to the oven about 1 hour from the end of the cooking time of the lamb.

For best results and top I-know-what-I'm-doing marks, don't carve the lamb straight away but allow it to rest for 10 minutes, lightly covered with foil. Serve with the hot, crisp potatoes, and don't forget the gravy ...

Caramelised Apple Pork Steaks with Brie and Cider Sauce

Serves 2-4
Preparation time: 10 minutes
Cooking time: 20 minutes

Some of you will, I am sure, be no stranger to Brie and cider, a magical combination that instantly transports you to woodland groves, country pubs and those idyllic days of scrumping for apples before being caught by the village vicar and being given a good spanking ... Sorry, I was miles away. Where were we? Oh, Brie and cider with freshly scrumped caramelised apples — you'd be a fool not to give it a go.

4 pork escalopes, chops or loin steaks
4 oz / 100 g Brie cheese, cut into pieces
2 oz / 50 g unsalted butter
2 oz / 50 g brown sugar
2 large apples (cooking apples are best, but any will do)
2 tablespoons crème fraîche
4 tablespoons cider (dry or sweet)
1 tablespoon fresh sage, washed and finely chopped
salt and freshly ground black pepper
slug of olive oil

Peel and core the apples, then chop them into eighths. Melt the butter in a frying pan over a gentle heat and add the sugar, stirring the two together. As the sugar begins to dissolve and the butter bubble a little, add the apple segments and cook them, stirring occasionally, for 5 minutes, or until thoroughly golden and tender. Remove the apple from the pan with a slotted spoon and place it in a foil-covered bowl to keep warm.

Add the oil to the pan and heat over a moderate heat. Add

the pork steaks and cook them for 5-6 minutes on each side, ensuring the oil is hot before you add the meat. Remove the steaks and place them on warmed plates. Quickly add the pieces of Brie to the pan and heat together with the cider. When the Brie dissolves into the cider, remove the pan from the heat and stir in the chopped sage, crème fraîche and seasoning. Cover the steaks with the caramelised apples and top each with a spoonful of the cider and Brie sauce.

Voluptuous Veg, Erotic Eggs and Sinful Sides

The world of veg is an incredibly diverse jungle of smells and tastes, filled to the brim with the most bizarre sights one could ever imagine. We like to believe – since veg is ever so good for us – that as a food source it is as free from controversy as a Trappist monk. But many veg are renowned for having mysterious and powerful aphrodisiac properties, and perhaps part of this legend stems from the fact that so many veg look indescribably saucy. However, we also know that vegetables (along with fruit and nuts) are packed full of vitamins and minerals and that a regular and varied supply helps keep our bodies healthy and our minds alert. Ergo, for those at the back, veg makes us feel good as well as looking obscenely colourful and sometimes perversely gnarled on your plate ... SO EAT LOADS! You should have veg with every meal, either as a main or a side – and I guarantee your potential beau will be well impressed with your healthy habits.

Eggs, meanwhile, are where it all began. They're packed full of protein – nature's edifying recharge facility – and are at their best kept as light and fluffy as possible (when we're talking about the ones from birds) and in their simplest form to bring out the flavour (when we're talking about the ones from fish). As a symbol of reproduction, sex and fertility, eggs have no substitute. Go to work (in the most euphemistic sense) on one, and always remember to buy free-range.

Imam Bayildi

Serves 2
Preparation time: 15 minutes
Cooking time: 50 minutes (total)

This dish — which means, literally, 'the priest has fainted' and is of purportedly Turkish origin — was named in honour of a village Imam (the Muslim equivalent of the parish vicar) who, after a hard day of abstinence, praying and little else, came home to find this delight waiting for him. The tender chunks of aubergine represented a little too much pleasure for him it seems, and he passed out, or so the saying goes. My theory is that the pine kernels, those little devils, whipped him up into such a frenzy of temptation that his brain couldn't cope and simply shut down. Let's hope yours doesn't — give in to temptation, I say. It generally works out as being much easier.

1 large aubergine
1/8 pt / 75 ml olive oil
1 white onion
1 green pepper, deseeded and chopped
2 large garlic cloves
6 oz / 150 g tomatoes
1 tablespoon fresh parsley, chopped (with a few sprigs to garnish)
1 tablespoon pine kernels
1 teaspoon brown sugar
juice of ½ lemon (with the other half saved to garnish)
salt and freshly ground black pepper

Prepare by heating the oven to 190°C / 375°F and skinning the tomatoes by immersing them in freshly boiled water for 1 minute, then pulling off the skins. Remove as many of the seeds as you can and chop the remaining flesh.

Slice the aubergine in half along its length and scoop out the flesh into a bowl. When doing this, leave a clear 2-cm margin of flesh behind, otherwise the skins will disintegrate when baked. This is where tradition states you're supposed to sprinkle the insides of the skins with salt and turn them upside down to drain away the 'bitter' juices, but I've never found this makes too much of a difference.

Heat half the oil in a saucepan over a moderate heat and add the onion, peeled and finely chopped, and the garlic, crushed. Add the aubergine flesh, chopped tomatoes, green pepper, lemon juice, sugar, parsley, pine kernels and a dash of salt and pepper. Reduce the heat and simmer the mixture for 15-20 minutes, until it begins to thicken. Remove the pan from the heat and spoon the filling into the aubergine shells. Place the shells side by side in a lightly greased baking dish. In a separate bowl, mix the remaining oil with an equal amount of water and a generous smattering of seasoning. Pour this mixture around (but not on) the aubergine halves, and bake them in an oven for 30 minutes.

This treat is splendid served both hot and cold with a couple of lemon wedges for squeezing and a little parsley for looks.

Nut Balls

Serves 2–4
Preparation time: 25 minutes
Cooking time: 25 minutes

Vegetarian Albondigas to you, these spicy spheres are zingy and tasty alternative to tapas meatballs and can be served up as a starter, a side or even as a main course. Such globular delights should really be handled as much as possible, so dispense with the cutlery for dipping and teasing fun. Ay! – I saw that: not too much of that sherry now, or you won't make it to dessert.

2 tablespoon ground almonds
2 tablespoon ground hazelnuts
2 tablespoons ground pecan nuts
4 tablespoons fresh white breadcrumbs
4 oz / 100 g Cheddar cheese, grated
1 large egg
4 tablespoons sherry (dry is best) – and have the bottle handy
1 small onion, finely sliced
1 red pepper, deseeded and sliced into tiny chunks
6-cm piece fresh ginger, peeled and grated
1 tablespoon fresh parsley, chopped
1 small red chilli, deseeded and finely chopped
salt and pepper to season
1 lemon, quartered to serve

In a big bowl mix all the nuts, breadcrumbs and cheese together (with your hands is best). In a separate bowl lightly beat together the egg and sherry, and mix in the onion, ginger, parsley, chilli and the pepper – which should be sliced up into tiny cubes or thin strips. Add this mixture to the nut and cheese mix, season the whole lot well and knead it all together.

The texture should be such that a half-fist sized ball should stay together in a cohesive lump. If the mixture is too dry and the ball simply falls apart, add sherry little by little. Remember, it's better to have too little moisture rather than too much, as the latter can be quite difficult to rectify afterwards. When the mix has a decent consistency, grease a baking tray and shape ten equal sized balls from the mixture to place upon it.

Put the balls in the oven and turn it on (they need to heat up slowly rather than roast). Keep the heat low (180°C / 350°F) and cook for 25 minutes. Alternatively, they can be fried in a little oil over a low heat for a similar length of time.

Delicious served with a wedge of lemon for squeezing and a cooling sauce – perversely, tomato ketchup is excellent.

Garlic and Basil Butter Mush-Tof Medley

Serves 2 (or 4 as a starter or a side)
Preparation time: 10 minutes
Cooking time: 10 minutes

Really easy and simple while still lightly meaty and awakening. The tiny, bulbous headed mushrooms complement the straight arithmetical squares of the tofu, with a smattering of illicit green. The Mediterranean taste means it goes beautifully with loads of pasta, fish and rice dishes, while the ginger provides a cleansing aphrodisiac zing.

8 oz / 225 g button mushrooms, washed
8 oz / 225 g smoked tofu, cut into squares of ½ inch / 1 cm sides
4 oz / 100 g unsalted butter
4-cm piece fresh ginger, peeled and grated or minced
4 garlic cloves, peeled and crushed
2 tablespoons fresh basil, chopped

Melt the butter in a heavy frying pan over a low heat. Add the ginger and crushed garlic to the pan, and fry very gently for 3 minutes. Add the mushrooms and cook for a further 5 minutes, until the mushrooms are soft. Add the tofu and turn up the heat just a touch, stirring carefully so as not to break the tofu cubes, for a further 2 minutes, then stir in the chopped basil. Serve with a slotted spoon, but use a tablespoon for extra buttery juice. A little squeeze of lemon juice, just at the end of the cooking time, provides an optional sharpening of the flavour.

Nicely Spicy Sweet Pot and Bean Pasties

Serves 2
Preparation time: 20 minutes
Cooking time: 30 minutes

Sweet potato is undoubtedly one of the best things ever and should be devoured with gusto on every possible occasion. For those without a desire for the elaborate, a heap of the stuff mashed with just a little butter, makes a tasty and colourful side dish for just about any meal. It works equally impressively as a main if mixed with something supercharging and spicy – try it in a curry, or in these pasties, revved up and ready to go in a hamper packed for a clandestine picnic. Make sure you go somewhere with plenty of hay to roll around in after lunch.

8 oz / 225 g shortcrust pastry
1 large sweet potato, peeled and chopped into chunks
2 oz / 50 g French beans, chopped
1 small white onion, peeled and finely chopped
1 garlic clove
2-cm piece fresh ginger, peeled and minced or grated
1 tablespoon fresh coriander
½ teaspoon chilli powder
½ teaspoon tumeric
½ teaspoon cumin
¼ teaspoon English mustard powder
slug of olive oil
1 egg

Bring a large pan of water to the boil and add the chunks of sweet potato. Simmer for 10 minutes until the flesh is tender. While it cooks, mix the chilli, tumeric, cumin and mustard powder together in a small bowl, and turn the oven on to heat to 200°C / 400°F.

After 10 minutes, drain the sweet potato and allow it to cool. Heat the olive oil in a large saucepan over a medium heat, crush in the garlic, add the onion and fry them until soft. Next, add the ginger and the spice mixture. Continue to fry for a further minute, until the scent of the spices begins to waft vigorously from the pan. Add the sweet potato and beans, and 2 tablespoons of cold water, and continue to cook for a further 5 minutes: by now you should have a nicely mashy mixture, with the green beans cooked and prominent. Chop the coriander and stir it in to the mixture, then remove it from the heat.

While the sweet potato mixture cools, divide the pastry into four pieces and roll each bit out into a circle on a lightly floured surface: it doesn't have to be an exact circle – near enough will do. Put one of the pastry circles on a lightly greased baking tray. Place a large spoonful of the cooled mixture on the centre of each pastry circle, adding more if there are any leftovers. Dampen the edges of each piece of pastry and bring the edges up to the top to make a Cornish-pasty-like shape. Repeat with the 3 remaining circles.

Finally beat the egg and brush it over the pasties. Place them in the oven for 20 minutes, or until they are a crisp golden brown.

Orange, Yellow and Ginger Vegetables

Serves 4 as a side
Preparation time: 15 minutes
Cooking time: 30 minutes

Not only are carrots and parsnips ridiculously good for you, they also contain trace quantities of myristic acid, which is found in abundant quantities in nutmeg and is believed to have aphrodisiac effects.

2 parsnips
4 carrots
2 oz / 50 g butter
4-cm piece of fresh ginger
nutmeg
1 tablespoon fresh parsley, finely chopped
2 teaspoons caster sugar
juice of 1 lemon

Wash and peel the carrots and parsnips and slice them into thick pieces. Melt the butter in a large pan over a low heat and gently sauté the carrot and parsnip pieces for 4 minutes. Mince or grate the ginger into the pan, add a healthy grate of nutmeg, the lemon juice, and add enough water to just cover the veg.

Cover the pan with a well-fitting lid and allow the contents to simmer away for 20 minutes, by which time the carrots and parsnips should be tenderly soft and the liquid mostly evaporated. Increase the heat a little and spoon in the sugar, stirring and tossing the vegetables until they are coated with a glossy sheen. Serve sprinkled with a handful of finely chopped parsley and season to taste.

Sweet Glazed Shallots

Serves 2-4 as a side
Preparation time: 15 minutes
Cooking time: 20 minutes

The Romans were the first to realise that shallots and onions, as well as possessing a sharp and clinging smell and making you cry when you cut them, have a certain something in them that can invigorate, as Martial put it, 'your tired old member'. Perhaps Casanova would have had a different nickname if he'd eaten fifty of these in the bath every morning, but they make for a refreshingly simple side dish, perfect for a romantic roast.

1 lb / 500 g shallots
3 oz / 75 g butter
2 teaspoons brown sugar
2 teaspoons English mustard powder
paprika
parsley to garnish

Allow the oven to heat to 180°C / 375°F. Peel the shallots, cut them in half and lay them, flat side down, in a baking dish. Melt the butter in a pan over a gentle heat and add the sugar and mustard powder, and finally ¼ pt / 100 ml of water, stirring until just below boiling. Pour this mixture over the shallots and dust the tops with a sprinkling of paprika.

Place the baking tray in the oven for 20 minutes, or until the shallots are richly glazed and glossy. Served from a heated dish, garnished with a little parsley.

Creamy Coriander Carrots

Serves 2-4 as a side
Preparation time: 10 minutes
Cooking time: 15 minutes

Glossy carrots, all creamy and with coolly spicy coriander mixed in, make a bright and tasty side dish for any meal. These have a tiny sprinkling of nutmeg for a warmer, invigorating flavour.

1 lb / 500 g baby carrots
2 tablespoons single cream
2 tablespoons fresh coriander, chopped
nutmeg
fresh black pepper

Wash and trim the carrots and place them in a large saucepan with enough water to just cover them. Heat until the water begins to boil, then cover the pan, reduce the heat and simmer the carrots for 10 minutes. Then remove the lid, turn up the heat and vigorously boil the water until it has all been absorbed or has evaporated, shaking the pan to prevent the carrots from burning. Remove the pan from the heat and stir in the coriander, cream and a generous twist of pepper. Transfer them to a warm serving dish, sprinkle over a little nutmeg (¼ teaspoon) and serve.

Funky Porcini Risotto

Serves 2
Preparation time: 15 minutes
Cooking time: exactly 22 minutes!

Fungi Porcini season is an exciting time in Italy. The arrival of these large and strangely grotesque woodland mushrooms sends the inhabitants of the villages in the undulating north into a frenzy. And although they might not be much to look at, the intense flavour of these delicacies is said to pack a powerful aphrodisiac punch. For those who know they make the winter – and the winter nights – worth waiting for.

4 oz / 100 g dried porcini mushrooms
1 tablespoon extra virgin olive oil
1 shallot, finely chopped
6 oz / 150 g Arborio rice
35 ml / half-bottle sherry (dry is best)
2 tablespoons fresh thyme
2 oz / 50 g Parmesan cheese
good vegetable stock cubes or 1¾ pints / 1 litre vegetable stock

Add the dried porcinis to a litre of vegetable stock in a saucepan. Bring it to the boil, then immediately reduce the heat so it simmers just below boiling point.

In a large, heavy-based saucepan, heat the olive oil over a medium heat. Add the shallot and sauté for 3 minutes, then add the rice and continue to cook for 3 minutes, stirring well to prevent the rice from sticking to the bottom. Pour in the sherry – leaving you enough left over for a couple of glasses – and continue to stir and cook until it has all been absorbed. Ladle in a couple of spoons of the hot stock, then reduce the heat under the rice slightly until the mixture is just simmering.

Remove the porcinis from the stock with a slotted spoon. Coarsely chop them and add them to the rice, stirring them in well. Continue to add ladlefuls of the stock every few minutes until the rice seems to have absorbed all it can. The Italians say the perfect risotto cooking time is 22 minutes, and that the rice should be removed from the heat as soon as it is *al dente* – it's simpler to serve it up when it is good and creamy, with the thyme and Parmesan stirred in just at the end of the cooking period, and with salt and pepper added to taste. Not too many side dishes needed for this one as it's so rich and creamily wholesome – just a few hunks of crusty bread.

As porcinis are expensive, it's best to save the remaining infused stock for another occasion. Also, for those with electric hobs and those with a irrational fear of having to clean risotto rice from the bottom of the pan with paint-stripper who may be reading, if you keep the heat really low you should be all right. But if the worst happens and you find a layer of black crusted semolina at the base of your pan don't panic. Simply transfer the contents to a new saucepan and continue cooking.

Asparagus, Red Pepper and Olive Quiche

Serves 2 (perhaps with some left over for lunch tomorrow)
Preparation time: 20 minutes
Cooking time: 40 minutes

Ah, asparagus — nature's teasingly penis-shaped joke. Asparagus is beautiful if lightly fried and drizzled with a little melted butter and nothing more than a fresh smattering of black pepper. But happy camping picnickers may want to try this stupidly easy quiche, however, crammed as it is with flavoursome olives and peppers.

1 x 10 inch / 26 cm part-baked pastry shell
3 large eggs
½ pint / 280 ml single cream
1 medium white onion, finely chopped
1 red pepper, deseeded and finely sliced
2 oz / 50 g asparagus tips
2 oz / 50 g pitted green olives
2 oz / 50 g Cheddar cheese, grated
2 tablespoons Parmesan cheese
1 tablespoon plain flour
2 oz / 50 g butter
nutmeg
salt and freshly ground black pepper

Preheat the oven to 190°C / 375°F, and melt 1 oz (25 g) of the butter in a small pan over a low heat. Add the chopped onion to the butter and allow it to soften and discolour, stirring occasionally. When soft, remove the onion from the pan with a slotted spoon and put aside for later.

In a bowl, lightly whisk the eggs and cream together. Add ½

a teaspoon of salt, a good few twists of black pepper and a brisk grate of nutmeg — no more than ½ a teaspoon's worth. Scoop up a little of the mixture in a cup and add the flour, stirring until smooth, then pour this back into the bowl and mix well.

Arrange the asparagus tips, the whole olives and the deseeded and sliced red pepper in the pastry shell, ensuring an even spread of vegetables. Pour the cream, eggs and flour mixture over the top and sprinkle with the grated Parmesan and Cheddar. Cut the remaining butter into tiny chunks and sprinkle these over the cheese. Place the pastry shell directly on the middle oven shelf and bake for 25 minutes, then turn the heat down a notch and bake at 180°C / 350°F for a further 10-15 minutes, or until the surface of the quiche is a deliciously glossy golden brown. Great both hot as an invigorating midday meal, and cold as an *al fresco* appetiser.

Perfect Pesto Genovese

Serves 2
Preparation time: 5 minutes
Cooking time: N/A

Pesto is a favourite for a quick and invigorating meal. The pine nuts are the key to this Genovese recipe, their coarse, warming flavour making this a simple aphrodisiac snack when a spoonful is stirred through fresh, cooked pasta.

1 oz / 25 g pine kernels
1 oz / 25 g Parmesan cheese
2 garlic cloves
1 tablespoon good white breadcrumbs
3 tablespoons extra virgin olive oil
3 tablespoons fresh basil (Genovese basil if you can get it)

Peel and roughly chop the garlic cloves and throw them in a food processor with all the other ingredients. Whizz them all together in 10-second bursts until the mixture has a consistent yet coarse texture. Serve with fresh pasta, or spread it on a pizza base as a delicious alternative to tomato sauce.

Simple Truffle Eggs

Serves 2
Preparation time: 10 minutes
Cooking time: 6 minutes

Few people have time for truffles because they consider them ludicrously expensive and complicated to deal with. True, they are more expensive than your average tuber – but then your average tuber is the potato. However, like most fantastic delicacies, connoisseurs will tell you that the most simple preparation is also the best, with fantastic and unlikely concoctions best left to the professionals. If you do get hold of some and you want to investigate their legendary aphrodisiac properties, do so scientifically with them nestled in a control sample of eggs, cooked as slowly and as fluffily as possible.

4 medium eggs
2 oz / 50 g dark or white truffles
1 tablespoon crème fraîche
salt and fresh black pepper

To keep the eggs and truffles moist, the best way to cook this dish is to heat the eggs over hot water, in the same way you might melt chocolate. So, bring a large water-filled saucepan to the boil. In a second saucepan (which needs to be slightly smaller so it can sit in the boiling water) gently whisk together the eggs and season lightly. Slice the truffles and add them to the mixture. Place the smaller saucepan over the boiling water and stir the mixture until it begins to thicken – this may seem like it takes forever, but in reality it only takes 5-6 minutes: just make sure you keep stirring the whole time.

Remove the thickening mixture from the heat and stir in the crème fraîche. Serve immediately, spread thickly on toast.

Vodka Caviar Fettuccine

Serves 2
Preparation time: 10 minutes (unless you're making
your own pasta ...)
Cooking time: 10 minutes

*Since you've gone and got some caviar and now think you're
Mr or Mrs Swank, you may as well go the whole hog and whip
up something delicious with it. Caviar – OK, salmon roe in this
recipe as we're not that classy yet – has a long and cheekily
sexual relationship with ribbony and twistable pastas like
fettuccine and linguine, and works incredibly well with vodka,
which you should have safely stored in the freezer (in a plastic
bottle, as glass can crack) – with shot glasses to hand – to
make your cooking experience a thoroughly smooth affair.*

8 oz / 225 g fresh fettuccine
2 oz / 50 g salmon roe
1/3 pt / 250 ml single cream
zest of ½ a lemon
1 garlic clove
1 oz / 25 g unsalted butter
2 tablespoons grated Parmesan cheese
2 tablespoons vodka (or, alternatively, Marsala)
1 tablespoon fresh chives, finely chopped
slug of olive oil
salt and freshly ground black pepper

Heat the cream in a heavy-based saucepan over a moderate
heat, adding the garlic clove – leaving it whole but squished
with the back of a heavy knife – and lemon zest and bringing
the pan to the boil. Reduce the heat slightly but continue to
allow the cream to boil until it has thickened and reduced by
about a third of its original volume.

Remove the garlic clove and lemon zest with a slotted spoon and add the butter to the cream, cut into chunks, and the grated Parmesan cheese, and whisk the mixture lightly until smooth. Allow the contents of the pan to simmer for 2 minutes before removing it from the heat and stirring in a good two tablespoons of the vodka, and a big twist of pepper.

Meanwhile, bring a large saucepan of water to the boil, adding a good pinch of salt and a drizzle of olive oil. Add the fettuccine (or your favourite pasta – this will work just as well with something like linguine) and boil until al dente after 4 minutes – or as packet instructions if cooking dried pasta.

Drain the pasta, place it in a large bowl and stir in the salmon roe and the cream sauce. Serve immediately whilst piping hot, with a handful of chopped chives topping each plate.

Potato and Egg Breasts

Serves 2
Preparation time: 20 minutes (including potato cooking time)
Cooking time: 20 minutes

Well, OK, these made it in because they look rude. There's something delightfully naughty about a baked egg nestling inside an inviting and crisp potato basket – but why stop there? With the potato nest as a base you can make a tempting breast out of any bakeable leftovers. Juicy tomato nipple, anyone? Also the best way to bake eggs (healthy, dontchaknow?) for all those non-ramekin owners out there.

1 lb / 500 g floury potatoes, e.g., King Edward
2 large eggs
1-2 tablespoons semi-skimmed milk
1 oz / 25 g unsalted butter
2 oz / 50 g Cheddar or Gruyère cheese, grated

Preheat the oven to 200°C / 400°F. Bring a large pan of water to the boil and add the washed potatoes, cut into quarters. You can peel them first or cook them in their skins, which will fall off after they're cooked – whichever you find most convenient.

After 20 minutes the potatoes should be tender and mashable. Drain them well and leave them in the pan with a tea towel covering them for 2 minutes. Then add the butter, milk and a twist of seasoning (a little salt and plenty of pepper). The mash consistency you're aiming for is smooth but firm – i.e., a spoonful of it, lifted from the bowl, should stay on the spoon. The best way to achieve this is to add the butter and milk little by little so you don't go overboard.

Grease a baking tray and divide the mash into two mounds upon it. Press down the centre of each mound with your fingers, to form a well. Carefully (yolk intact now ...) break an egg into each well and top each egg with a sprinkling of grated cheese. Place the baking tray in the oven for 20 minutes – or until the eggs are thoroughly set and the potato is beginning to turn a slightly crispy gold. Serve hot with a wry and cheeky smile.

Vegetarian Green Curry (with Jasmine Rice, of course)

Serves 2
Preparation time: 20 minutes (including marinating time)
Cooking time: 20 minutes (including time to cook rice)

Green curry is a classic tube opener. Sorry, that came out all wrong. The kaffir lime and the ginger in green curry paste, and the handful of coriander thrown in at the end, all combine to give a hot yet cleansing sensation, guaranteed to clear the most stubborn blocked nose and to revitalise the sleepiest of heads. For a non-vegetarian alternative, if you're feeling a bit flush, use 8 oz / 225 g of jumbo king prawns instead of the tofu.

8 oz / 225 g smoked tofu, cut into small cubes
4 oz / 100 g bamboo shoots
4 oz / 100 g beansprouts
2 tablespoons dark soy sauce
½ pint / 280 ml coconut milk (you can also used creamed coconut with hot water)
1 tablespoon green curry paste
1 green pepper, deseeded and cut into strips
1 tablespoon peas (frozen is fine)
slug of vegetable oil
1 tablespoon fresh coriander, roughly chopped
1 spring onion, finely sliced

While you chop up the pepper and bamboo shoots, allow the tofu cubes to marinate in the soy sauce for 20 minutes or so. Heat the oil in a wok or saucepan over a medium heat and add the green curry paste, frying it for 1 minute. Add half the coconut milk and the drained tofu, green pepper and bamboo shoots. Continue to cook these at the same temperature for 5 minutes, stirring gently and occasionally, taking care not to break the tofu cubes. Add the remaining coconut milk, the peas and the beansprouts. When the curry comes to the boil, reduce the heat and allow it to simmer away for 10 minutes.

Just before serving, stir in the chopped coriander, and serve in bowls garnished with a little sprinkle of chopped spring onion. This isn't a curry unless it's served with steaming hot traditional Thai jasmine rice that you can buy from any good supermarket.

Basil Dribbling Oil

Preparation time: 20 minutes

Give tomato and mozzarella a new lease of life, or in hard times hand this stuff out as a present – either way you're on to a winner.

4 tablespoons (2 handfuls) fresh basil leaves
4 sprigs rosemary, chopped
17 fl oz / 500 ml bottle olive oil

Pour the olive oil into a saucepan over a low heat. Bring it to just below its boiling point – i.e., it will be hot but hardly bubbling. Add the rosemary, tear in the basil and make sure the oil covers them. Allow the oil to infuse with the herbs' flavour for twenty minutes.

In the meantime, wash out a suitably sized glass bottle with boiling water – ideally, though, use the bottle from which the oil originated, as long as it is made of glass. Allow the oil to cool, then strain it through a sieve and carefully decant it into the bottle. This is best kept refrigerated and will keep for about a month – though by then you'll probably have used it all up.

Chilli and Garlic Dipping Oil

Preparation time: 30 minutes

Probably best not to drizzle this one over salads as it has a kick as wicked as you want to make it: more chillies, more oomph. It's amazing as a dipper for all sorts of things – especially chicken – and gives a fiery zing to your favourite romantic pasta.

8 large garlic cloves
10 red chillies
17 fl oz / 500 ml bottle olive oil

Finely slice the chillies – there's no need to deseed them – and bash each clove of garlic with the back of a knife to squish it open. From then on use the same process as for the Basil Dribbling Oil: simply heat the oil, add the chilli and garlic and allow them to infuse the oil – this time for a little longer. Cool, strain and decant into a clean bottle.

For a fearsomely stronger oil, stuff the chilli slices and garlic cloves back into the bottle with the oil (in this case, the oil should be kept for two weeks or so – otherwise it can really be used indefinitely).

Buttery Mash with Parsley and Nutmeg

Serves 2 as a side
Preparation time: 10 minutes (depending on how fast you peel)
Cooking time: 20 minutes

There are times when mash is a must: a simple and unrefined mash, that is, with absolutely no frills. Other times, well, we need something to rekindle our love affair with the humble spud. We need to be reminded just how creamy, sultry and smooth she really is. Sometimes all it takes is a big dollop of mustard, but for the potato to really show off her curves she needs silky cream, a lovely fresh egg, a delectable dollop of butter and the warming, sexy hit of nutmeg.

10 oz / 250 g floury potatoes, e.g., King Edward
1 egg
2 oz / 50 g unsalted butter
1 tablespoon fresh parsley
1-2 tablespoons semi-skimmed milk
1 tablespoon single cream
nutmeg, salt and freshly ground black pepper

Simply peel, halve and boil the potatoes for 15-20 minutes or until they're soft and mashable. Drain them well, and leave them for a minute in the pan with a tea towel over them to absorb the steam. Add the butter, milk, cream, chopped parsley, a good twist of salt and pepper, and mash it all together until it has a smooth creamy consistency. Grate in about ½ a teaspoons' worth of nutmeg, stir it in well and keep it all warm until ready to serve.

Hannah Hills' Lovely Spicy Porridge Breakfast

Serves 2 in bed
Cooking time: 5-10 minutes

This is just what you need in the morning: something warm, moist and lusciously spicy. Cardamom, cinnamon and nutmeg are all renowned for brightening many a weary eye – and on no account forget the awesome aphrodisiac power of porridge, the strength-boosting cereal to beat all others.

8 oz / 225 g porridge oats
enough milk to cover the oats
1 banana
handful of raisins
5 cardamom pods
nutmeg
powdered cinnamon

Put the porridge oats into a pan and add enough milk to cover them. Add the chopped banana, raisins, cardamom pods, ¼ teaspoon of freshly grated nutmeg and ½ teaspoon of cinnamon powder. Bring to the boil and then cook over a low heat for 5-10 minutes until the porridge is heated through and has a nice consistency. Remove the cardamom pods and serve in a big bowl with two spoons.

Steve Willis' Savoury Vegetable Purse

Serves 2-4
Preparation time: 15 minutes
Cooking time: 35 minutes

Steve Willis is a cook of the highest order. Celebrate his dainty tubes, stuffed full of steaming cheesy goodness.

2 oz / 50 g margarine
good slug of olive oil
ten 12 x 6 inch sheets of filo pastry
8 oz / 225 g courgettes, thinly sliced
4 oz / 100 g French beans, cut in half
8 oz / 250 g broccoli, sliced
6 oz / 150 g feta cheese, cut into cubes
1 tablespoon fresh thyme, chopped
1 tablespoon fresh tarragon, chopped
1 egg, beaten
sea salt and freshly ground pepper

Preheat the oven to 190°C / 375°F. Prepare the vegetables by steaming them for 5-7 minutes – this will work well in a stackable steamer as you can do them all at once. Leave them to cool and melt the margarine in a pan over a very low heat. Add a good slug of olive oil and brush the mixture lightly over five of the filo sheets – then stack these on top of one another.

Shaking free any excess moisture, put the steamed vegetables in a bowl and mix in the cubed feta cheese. Season with a little salt, a big twist of pepper, and add the thyme and tarragon. Divide this mixture in half and spread one half of it over the surface of the stacked pastry, making sure there is a clear 2-inch margin of pastry spare around the edges. Roll the pastry into a tube from the long side (like a Swiss roll) and fold in the short edges. Brush the surface with the beaten egg and place the 'purse' seam side down on a well-greased baking tray.

Repeat the process with the other half of the veg mixture to make a second purse, and bake them both together for 30-35 minutes, or until the outside of the pastry is a crisp golden brown. Leave the purses alone for a couple of minutes before serving, sliced and garnished with a flower.

Delirious Desserts

After all that lot you may already be in a state of ecstatic frenzy and considering swiping everything onto the floor and indulging in a spot of impromptu dessert straight from your imagination on the dining table. But behave! Try something light, tasty and refreshing before retiring to the boudoir. Rude desserts should be either palette-cleaning – like an ice-cold sorbet or fresh ice cream – or fun, sticky and messy. Spoon-feed one another – or dispense with the cutlery altogether and let your fingers and lips do the work.

Chocolate Dicking and Lipping Sauce

Serves ... just 2
Preparation time: 15 minutes

For food foreplay you simply must find yourself a decent dicking and lipping sauce. Or should that be licking and dipping? Whatever — this one will stay semi-liquid and can be kept in the fridge for a week. It's nice on toast, better off toes, and deserves a quick blast in the microwave and a stir to get it good and gooey before use.

8 oz / 225 g dark, bitter or cooking chocolate (the best quality)
2 tablespoons golden syrup
2 tablespoons espresso coffee
½ pint / 300 ml single cream
1 tablespoon dark rum

Break the chocolate into pieces and put them in a heavy-based saucepan with the golden syrup, cream and coffee. Heat the pan very gently, ideally suspended over another pan ¼-full of gently simmering water. Stir continuously until all the chocolate has melted, the consistency is even and the texture glossy. Stir in the rum and remove the pan from the heat.

Use immediately, nice and warm, or store refrigerated in an airtight container for up to a week, mixing well and heating gently before use.

Spotted Dick

Serves 4
Preparation time: 20 minutes
Cooking time: 2 hours

Because it would be rude not to.

8 oz / 225 g self-raising flour
4 oz / 100 g raisins
4 oz / 100 g lightly salted butter (or unsalted and a pinch of salt)
2 oz / 50 g castor sugar

Fold a large square of baking parchment or greaseproof paper so it is double thickness and lay it on a baking tray. Take a little chunk of the butter and melt it in a pan over a low heat. Brush or smear it all over the parchment.

Sieve the flour into a bowl, cut the butter into small chunks and mix it into the flour with your hands. Mix in the sugar and raisins, then knead in 4 or 5 tablespoons of water until you have a soft dough. Remember it's best to add too little water to start with, rather than put in too much initially.

On a lightly floured surface, roll out the dough into a short, thick cylinder, or into whatever cylindrical-shaped object takes your fancy. I can hear your dirty little mind ticking away – go on, just do it: it will look like one. Place the dick on the greased paper and wrap it securely but loosely, sealing the ends with string or rubber bands. Place the dick package in a steamer with a well-fitting lid and steam for 2 hours.

Serve with lashings of custard, naturally.

Simple Mango Sorbet

Serves 4
Preparation time: 15 minutes (plus 1 hour to freeze)

Mangoes are rude enough without having anything else done to them and I can recommend one for dessert au naturel as eating them is such a naughtily messy affair. Ideally they should be slit open down their lengths with a sharp knife and burrowed into with hungry teeth and lips, which results in the syndrome known as Excessively Dribbly Chin. If you're feeling a little more sophisticated, try this simple sorbet – a breeze to rustle up and it contains a shot of gin for an extra little something.

2 lb / 1 kg ripe mango
2 tablespoons demerara sugar
2 tablespoons gin
12 ice cubes
salt

Simply peel the mangos, remove the stones and pulp the flesh in a blender together with the sugar and 1½ pints / 750 ml water. Add the gin, ice cubes and a pinch of salt and whizz it all together until the consistency is rough but even. Pour it into a frozen metal container (or, failing that, a Tupperware box) and freeze for one hour. Unlike ice cream, the formation of ice crystals is a must for sorbet, so there's no need to keep taking it out to stir, but give the sorbet a good mash before serving.

Champagne Ice Cream

Serves 2 with some to spare
Preparation time: 20 minutes (plus 1 hour to freeze)

If there's one drink most commonly associated with romance it has to be ... no, not tequila, although too much of it can make you think you're in love. A crisp and light champagne ice cream is just the thing to clean the palette and show that a tender romantic soul simmers behind that tough, professional chef exterior of yours ...

½ pint / 300 ml single cream
½ pint / 300 ml whipped cream
2 egg yolks
2 oz / 50 g caster sugar
zest of 1 lemon
2 flutes of champagne

Heat together the single cream, sugar, egg yolks and lemon zest in a heavy saucepan over a low heat, and stir continuously until the mixture comes to the boil. Remove the zest with a slotted spoon and remove the pan from the heat. When the mixture has cooled, fold in the whipped cream and the champagne. Transfer to an ice cream maker, turn it on and let it go about its business. If you do not have such a device, place the mixture in a pre-frozen metal container (or Tupperware box). Put the container in the freezer for an hour, removing it every 15 minutes to stir well with a whisk – this is to stop ice crystals forming, which will ruin the texture.

Serve with wafers, the last of the champagne, and eat lovingly from spoons, fingers, thighs and navels.

Coffee Ice Cream

Serves 4
Preparation time: 20 minutes (plus 1 hour to freeze)

'Back to my place for coffee ice cream?' isn't an arrangement of words you hear all that often – be the first to try it out with this smooth, bitter and rich wake-up call.

1 pint / 600 ml single cream
4 oz / 100 g caster sugar
4 egg yolks
2 tablespoons Kahlua
2 teaspoons vanilla essence
1 small cup espresso coffee
salt

Lightly whisk together the egg yolks, sugar and a pinch of salt. In a separate saucepan mix the cream, vanilla essence, coffee and Kahlua. Gradually add this coffee-cream mixture to the egg yolks, stirring continuously. Heat this mixture in a bowl or saucepan over another saucepan of simmering water, stirring continuously until the mixture begins to thicken a little – when ready it should be thick enough to coat the back of a spoon. Allow the mixture to cool and transfer it to the chilled bowl of an ice cream maker – let it do its stuff until the ice cream has set. Alternatively, if you don't own such a machine, freeze the mixture in a Tupperware box for 1 hour, removing it every 15 minutes to give it a good whisk.

For an extra cool touch, serve scooped into bowls, garnished with a sprinkling of coffee beans and a sprig of mint.

Honey and Lemon Baked Figs

Serves 4
Preparation time: 10 minutes
Cooking time: 20 minutes

Figs are one of the world's oldest symbols of fertility, procreation and rampant sexual longing, and are thought to have been Cleopatra's favourite snack. In fact, they are one of the oldest known plants in the world, and occupy a pedestal in many countries as a powerful sexual stimulant. Enjoy them baked, and be thankful that, in this country, they don't throw them at weddings.

6 figs
4 tablespoons clear runny honey
juice and zest of 1 lemon

Heat the oven to 200°C / 400°F. In a bowl cover the figs with the honey, add the lemon juice and zest, and mix the whole lot up so the figs are well coated. Pour the figs out into a baking dish, separating the fruits from one another, and drizzle any residual honey and lemon mix over them. Place the baking dish in an oven and cook for 20 minutes. Serve steaming hot with a scoop of vanilla ice cream or some crème fraîche.

Quetzalcoatl Cox's Chocolate Mousse

Serves 4 (or a chocoholic 2)
Preparation time: 1 hour (and 2 hours for it to set)

The Aztecs worshipped the sun god Quetzalcoatl and would celebrate their love for him with cocoa beans. They couldn't get enough of it and any old religious ceremony was a good enough excuse to whip out the chocolate. Opening new stepped pyramid? Let's have some chocolate. Sacrificing virgins? Ooh, go on then – just a couple of chunks for me. Unfortunately the herby concoction they made with cocoa was, to the Western palette, quite rank. I hope you'll find this recipe for a rich, decadent mousse has brought chocolate in from the cold days of Montezuma's revenge ...

IMPORTANT: As this dessert contains uncooked eggs it is not suitable for pregnant women, very young children, the elderly and anyone considered particularly susceptible to infection or disease.

8 oz / 225 g best quality chocolate (your choice of milk, cooking or dark – but always buy the best quality stuff available)
4 oz / 100 g unsalted butter
2 tablespoons liquid black instant coffee
2 tablespoons brandy
4 eggs
2 tablespoons caster sugar

Separate the egg whites and yolks and save both (how you go about this is up to you – I'd plump for the time-trusted method of using a cup and saucer: break the egg onto a saucer, place

116

the cup over the yolk and tip the saucer to drain off the white). Whisk together the yolks and 1 tablespoon of caster sugar in a bowl until thoroughly combined.

Break the chocolate into small pieces and melt it in a bowl or saucepan over another saucepan containing gently simmering water. Add the coffee and stir continuously until you have a smooth chocolate liquid. Chop the butter into pieces and gradually add it to the chocolate, beating the mixture with a whisk. When all the butter has melted and the mixture is smooth and even, add the egg yolk mixture, continuing to whisk constantly and patiently until the mixture thickens after 5 minutes or so. Remove the bowl from the heat, fold in the brandy with a spoon, and allow the mixture to cool.

While the chocolate cools, whisk the egg whites and the other tablespoon of sugar together until it forms soft fluffy peaks. You *could* do this by hand if you have wrists of steel and incredible patience: a better option is to use an electric whisk or beater. When the chocolate has cooled, fold in the egg whites with a spoon. Do this gently but thoroughly, trying to maintain the aerated structure of the egg white mix as much as possible.

When thoroughly combined, spoon the mixture into individual serving dishes. It won't seem like you have much per person but it is incredibly rich so a little should suffice. Place the dishes in the fridge to set for at least 2 hours, or overnight. Serve topped with a little grated chocolate, or a sprinkling of crushed Malteasers or Flake bars.

Guava Jelly
(For Rubbing 'Pon Your Belly)

Serves 6
Preparation time: 15 minutes
Cooking time: 40 minutes

Fans of Bob Marley will know all about the be-dreadlocked one's penchant for this particular Jamaican treat – and just where he'd like his damsel to rub it. A food treat for reggae relaxation like no other.

3 lbs / 1.5 kg guava
juice of 3 lemons
juice of 1 lime
2 tablespoons dark rum
granulated sugar

Wash the fruit and inspect the outside for any bruised or damaged bits, which you should then cut out and discard. Slice the whole fruits (no need to peel or core them) into thick chunks and place them in the largest pan you can find. Add the lemon and lime juices and enough cold water to cover the guava flesh entirely. Heat the water to boiling point, then turn the heat down a notch so the liquid simmers away. Leave it like this for 30 minutes, or until the liquid has reduced by about a third – the guava flesh should by now be soft and squishy.

Remove the pan from the heat and strain the guava flesh through a sieve, a jam bag or a clean nylon stocking, collecting the juice underneath. Really squidge up the guava so you get as much juice out as possible. The flesh can now be discarded. Measure the collected liquid in a measuring jug and return it to the pan. For every litre (2 pints) of liquid add 1 kg (2 lbs) of sugar. Bring the liquid back up to boiling point, stirring it up to dissolve all the sugar. Add the rum and boil vigorously for a further 2-3 minutes, skimming any foam from the surface, until it develops a thick consistency – this stuff should set by itself, as guava contains plenty of pectin. Pour the liquid out into jelly moulds or glasses (which should be sparklingly clean or sterilised), cover with cling film and refrigerate for 1 hour. Lively up yourself and serve – spoons not strictly necessary.

Chocolate Strawberriexplosions

Serves 2-4
Preparation time: 1 hour

Strawberries are the nipples of the fruit world. They can be served up in a zillion different ways and every one of them is delightful. These chocolate explosions are, I would hope, something your partner has never experienced before. Persevere with the fiddlyness of injecting the little blighters and you might be in for a treat yourself later on ...

8 oz / 225 g fresh strawberries
8 oz / 225 g dark, bitter or cooking chocolate (the best quality chocolate available)
75 ml Grand Marnier or Cointreau

Preparing the strawberries is a delicate operation but an easy one if you kit yourself out well beforehand. You'll need as many toothpicks as you have strawberries, some polystyrene in a block, oh, and a syringe. If you don't have the latter you'll have to leave out the 'surprise' element, but if you don't have polystyrene to hand it's easy to improvise.

Wash the strawberries but leave them whole (with stalks intact), and spear each one with a cocktail stick through the stalk end. Melt the chocolate by breaking it into chunks in a saucepan, and placing this saucepan over another pan of gently simmering water. Mix the chocolate as it melts until it is completely smooth. Remove the chocolate from the heat and dip each strawberry into it, swirling each one as you do so, so that about half of every strawberry is covered with chocolate.

Leaving the strawberries resting on anything will spoil the effect, so to ensure the chocolate shell hardens intact, spear the cocktail sticks into a suitably yielding surface. What's that? You have a block of polystyrene right there? Perfect. Otherwise an old tissue box turned upside down, Blu-Tack or even a bar of soap should do the trick. Place the array of strawberries in the bottom of the refrigerator for at least twenty minutes (this will harden the shells).

Before serving, use a syringe to inject the centre of each strawberry with a squirt of Cointreau, Grand Marnier or your choice of liqueur, arrange them alluringly on a dish, and feel waves of warmth and satisfaction envelop you as your partner marvels at your culinary kudos.

Sanchia Lovell's Creamy Breasts

Serves 2
Preparation time: 30 minutes (but needs to set
for 2 hours)

*These are smooth, creamy, slightly wobbly and taste delicious.
Sanchia's panna cotta creations are pretty nice as well, are
surprisingly easy to prepare, and make for a visually enticing
romantic dessert.*

2 pints / 1.2 litres double cream
2 vanilla pods
3 gelatin leaves
6 fl oz / 150 ml full fat milk
6 oz / 150 g icing sugar
120 ml / 4 fl oz amaretto (or liqueur of choice)
6 oz / 150 g punnet of raspberries, washed

In a heavy-based saucepan heat 900 ml / 1½ pints of the cream
and the vanilla pods together until boiling. Simmer until the liquid
has reduced by a third of its volume. Remove the pods (carefully
– they'll be hot!), open them out with a sharp knife and scrape
their insides into the cream.

Meanwhile, soak the gelatin leaves in the cold milk for 15
minutes. Remove the gelatin and heat the milk until boiling.
Replace the gelatin and stir well until it has all dissolved. Pour the
milk through a sieve into the cream. Stir well and leave the mixture
to cool.

Whisk the icing sugar into the remaining cream and fold it
into the cooled cream mixture. Mix in the amaretto, setting a little
of it aside for later. Go on then, and a glass for yourself. Pour the
mixture into two moulds of roughly 200 ml volume (bowls will
do), and refrigerate for 2 hours at least to allow the mixture to
set. Turn out the bowls onto dessert plates, garnish with
raspberries, a drizzle of amaretto, and serve.

Honey Pie

Serves 2
Preparation time: 20 minutes
Cooking time: 35 minutes

Warming, sticky, fabulously nutty, slightly fruity and ridiculously simple, Honey Pie served with a good old scoop of vanilla ice cream is the ultimate dessert for the sweet of tooth.

8 oz / 250 g honey (clear is best)
6 oz / 175 g chopped pecans (or walnuts or almonds)
10 oz / 300 g shortcrust pastry (if using frozen make sure it's thawed)
6 tablespoons dark rum
2 tablespoons caster sugar
1 tablespoon semi-skimmed milk
yolk of 1 egg
zest of 1 lemon
zest of ½ orange

Preheat the oven to 200°C / 400°F. Heat the honey gently in a saucepan. When hot add the pecans (you can use walnuts, almonds or just about any nut, but pecans are the best) and orange and lemon zests and stir to coat the nuts well. Add the rum, stir well and remove the pan from the heat.

Halve the pastry and roll it out until it is thin enough to line a 20-cm pie-dish, or any similar sized ovenproof dish. Sprinkle the sugar over the pastry lining and spoon the sticky honey mixture on top. Roll the remaining pastry out to form the lid, seal the edges and decorate the top with any offcuts you may have. I don't recommend tiny pastry phalluses complete with shortcrust testicles, but spelling out 'I Love U' with those stray pieces will earn you instant Brownie points (as long as you mean it).

Finally, brush the lid with a gently whisked mixture of egg yolk and milk, pierce the lid with a knife in five or six places, and bake in the hot oven for 30-35 minutes, or until the pastry is golden brown.

As the honey filling retains its heat well, it's best to let the pie cool for 10 minutes before serving. Vanilla ice cream simply and absolutely a must.

Amorous Alcohol

'It provokes the desire,' as the porter says in Shakespeare's Scottish play, 'but it takes away the performance' – and he wasn't talking about Lady Macbeth's merkin. Dally with alcohol in moderation is the moral of the tale, because few people find themselves getting all amorous towards gibbering messes. Nonetheless, a drink or two can loosen inhibitions and, if combined with the right ingredients (good food, good people, good conversation), can spark off something special. Here are a few of the world's classics, from Ibiza to Lisbon, via Lagos and, er, Chepstow. The usual sensible advice of course applies: if driving, don't drink – plump instead for an invigorating smoothie, crammed with an arsenal of aphrodisiacs.

Black Velvet

Champagne is, of course, well known for its association with romance. Stout is a less obvious suspect, but my African correspondent assures me that the Nigerian-brewed variety of Guinness is widely used as a pre-coital lifesaver. Of course, that black stuff is twice the strength of the stout the rest of the world enjoys, but in the interests of cosmopolitanism — and because it tastes nice — try the combination as a romantic aperitif. Black Velvet: not just for New Year ...

Irish stout (such as Guinness or Murphy's)
champagne, chilled

Fill champagne flutes half full of stout. Top up with chilled champagne.

SeaSunAnd ... Sangria

Serves 4

Many an Ibizan holidaymaker will have felt themselves slipping into a sandy, happy dream after a jug of this stuff, with that hangover from the previous evening's exertions rapidly becoming nothing but a distant memory ... only for them to wake up hours later to find 'arse' written on their head in factor seventy-six sunblock. Finally the microfilm containing the recipe has been smuggled from Spain and we can enjoy this romantic, summer cooler in the relatively safe comfort of our own gardens.

1 bottle Rioja or similar red wine
50 ml Havana Club rum, or Bacardi
juice of 1 lime
2 oranges
1 lemon
ice

Cut the lemon and oranges into chunks and put them in a jug that will hold a litre of liquid. Add the lime juice and rum, and top up with wine. Serve over ice in glasses, with a wooden spoon in the jug so you can strain out the fruit.

Between the Sheets

Serves 2

A naughty, sharp and wonderfully strong cocktail classic that leaves little to the imagination.

juice of 1 lemon
50 ml brandy
50 ml triple sec
50 ml light or Havana Club rum

Pour all the ingredients into a cocktail shaker over plenty of ice. Shake well, strain into two cocktail glasses and serve garnished with a twist of lemon peel if you want to be *really* classy.

Brian O'Faolin's Portuguese Hard-On

Serves 2

My personal investigations into this concoction reveal it gets you drunk, but my note-taking from that evening seems to be illegible. Brian assures me it is a romantic drink, guaranteed to keep you up until the wee hours. You'll have to ask Brian himself about the name — I'm sure there are legal reasons why it can't be described here.

50 ml vodka
50 ml peach schnapps
lemonade

Fill tall glasses with ice, add equal measures of vodka and peach schnapps, and top up with lemonade — as simple as that.

Long, Slow, Comfortable Screw (Up Against A Cold, Hard Wall)

Serves 2

A much-maligned drink, harking back as it does to the days of 80s chic, if such a phrase isn't a complete oxymoron. However, anything with Galliano in it deserves a little respect, and this is no exception. Put on your best lounge suit ... and get screwing.

25 ml vodka
25 ml sloe gin
25 ml Southern Comfort
25 ml Galliano
25 ml amaretto
orange juice

Combine the alcoholic ingredients in a cocktail shaker and pour them over cold hard walls of ice in long glasses. Top up with orange juice and serve.

Screaming Orgasm

Serves 2

I'm not sure this one needs too much introduction. Guaranteed to produce an orgasm of the tastebuds, a Screaming Orgasm is delightfully smooth and seductive.

25 ml vodka
25 ml amaretto
25 ml Bailey's Irish Cream
25 ml Kahlua

Simply mix together all the ingredients and serve in whiskey tumblers over cracked or crushed ice.

Passion Fruit Bellini

Serves 4

The cool vibrant colour of passion fruit brings a much needed touch of love to this classic Italian champagne cocktail.

4 ripe passion fruit
50 ml Cointreau
1 bottle champagne

Halve the passion fruit and scoop the flesh into a sieve. Gently force the flesh through the sieve with a fork or spoon, collecting the resulting purée in a jug. Add a generous 50 ml of Cointreau to the purée and mix well. Dollop a tablespoon of the mixture into each glass — use champagne flutes for authenticity — top up with chilled champagne and serve.

Vanilla Brandy

Serves several

After-dinner liqueurs are a key ingredient in continental dining; the only problem, from a rude point of view, is that they make you feel like slipping off into a comfortable dream. Problem solved – drink the finest brandy and feel the full fruity aphrodisiac effects of dreamy smooth vanilla.

70 cl bottle good brandy
2 vanilla pods

Score the vanilla pods down the centre and put them straight into the brandy bottle, sealing it tightly. The brandy's flavour will improve with age, but will still be deliciously potent after about a week if you keep the bottle in a cool, dark place.

Vanilla Smoothie

Serves 4

OK – you're not all rampant alcoholics. It's just me. Here, then, is a concession to the sensible – a creamily stimulating smoothie, crammed full of vanilla goodness.

4 ripe bananas
½ pint / 300 ml natural yoghurt
½ pint / 300 ml semi-skimmed milk
1 vanilla pod
2 tablespoons runny honey
8 ice cubes

Peel and chop the bananas and put them in a food processor with the yoghurt, milk, honey and ice cubes. Cut the vanilla pod open and scrape all the seeds and sticky bits in, then whizz all the ingredients together until the consistency is even and the texture smooth. Serve immediately in long glasses.

Glühwein

Serves 4

A traditional drink for skiers and at Christmas, Glühwein is served up in the winter because of its warming and invigorating properties. However, any occasion is good enough for its spicy and zesty tang, and, with the infused taste of cloves, nutmeg, cinnamon and honey, its aphrodisiac properties make it perfect for a cosy night in.

1 bottle red wine
zest of 1 lemon
zest of 1 orange
4 whole cinnamon sticks
4 whole cloves
2 teaspoons freshly ground nutmeg
1 tablespoon honey

Find a square piece of muslin — or even a stocking, sterilised in boiling water — and tie up in it the cloves, cinnamon, lemon and orange zest and the nutmeg. Pour the bottle of wine into a large saucepan, add the muslin spice pouch, and heat the wine over a lowish heat, turning it down if it looks as if it'll start boiling. Add the honey and let it dissolve. Infuse the wine for 5 minutes, taking care not to let it boil, and serve warm. There should be enough spice in the pouch for another bottle, if the fancy takes you.

Hannah Lewis' Millennium Vodka

Serves several

Hannah made huge supplies of this for her millennium love-in, and has shared the coveted secret with Rude Food. A sweet and saucy one – definitely for special occasions only.

4 oz / 100 g good toffee
1 bottle vodka

Pour out a glass or two of the vodka or else you'll lose it when it dribbles down the sides of the bottle. Smash up the toffee into pieces small enough to fit through the bottleneck and push them in, topping up the bottle with the vodka you took out earlier and drinking any left over. Screw the lid on tightly, place the bottle in the dishwasher and run it through the hottest cycle, taking it out to give it a good shake halfway through. If at the end of the cycle the toffee isn't completely dissolved, run it through again.

For anyone without a dishwasher, simply stand the bottle, with the lid screwed on tightly, in a saucepan of water, simmering just below boiling point. Take the bottle out with oven gloves (it'll be hot!) and give it a good shake every few minutes. Remove and cool as soon as all the toffee has dissolved and the vodka is an even toffee-brown.

The A-Z of Rude Food

I hope those recipes were enough to give you that gentle push you were begging for, and that you're now sliding, hopelessly enraptured, down that slippery tunnel into a world filled with erotic recipes, wonderfully arousing aphrodisiacs and decadent, romantic meals. If, to complete your newfound skills as Mr or Miss Lover Lover (mmm), you're looking for a list of smarmy conversational ploys or smooth chat-up lines and seduction techniques, then I really can't help you, having never been too good at those myself. I can, however, hand over to you all I've discovered about rude food throughout my painstaking research. All that eating, all those frolics ... it was hard work, I can tell you. Please take this dictionary of filthy aphrodisiacs and rude food trivia and venture forth, with my blessing, into a new era of naughty food-filled sexperimentation ...

Aphrodite

Known by the Romans as Venus, Aphrodite was the goddess of love and beauty, lived on Mount Olympus (where she was married, rather dully, to Hephaestus, the god of craftsmen), and was the first winner of the coveted Golden Apple of Paris, beating off fierce competition from Athena (goddess of war and posters) and Hera (the queen of Olympus). Aphrodisiacs derive from her name because this was the name given to festivals the ancient Greeks would hold to celebrate her beauty. These festivals involved everyone feasting and then having free sex with the high priestesses from Aphrodite's temples around the country — a tactic the Church of England has yet to try in order to drum up trade. Though the festivals have, sadly, been long forgotten, Aphrodite's name lives on as a synonym for naughty, rude food.

Artichoke

These are as sensual to prepare as they are to eat. You can buy artichoke hearts in jars and tins, ready for use. Artichokes are extremely tasty if not incredible to behold. If you can get hold of fresh artichokes you'll have a world of fun peeling back the outer leaves, dipping your fingers into the delicate cup, and softly stroking the glowing heart within as it peers out from its prickly protection.

Asparagus

Eating one's first asparagus spear is something of an epiphany: the moment the bulbous head disappears between your lips, oozing globules of melted butter ... it's enough to make anyone come over all unnecessary. Rich in vitamins and minerals, asparagus is certainly a healthy treat as well as making for an erotic eating experience. Be warned, though: asparagus is guaranteed to make you smell. Did we get that at the back? Or was I being too coy? Your bodily fluids, semen and vaginal lubricant in particular, will smell of sweet, green vegetable matter – though this is not, as you might first think, entirely unpleasant.

Aubergine

A thoroughly indecent vegetable. Thick, phallic and arrogant, the aubergine makes a bold statement, yet inside, its flesh is crisp and pristine. When cooked it turns into a creamy morass that screams sex from the rooftops.

Avocado

Perhaps the sexiest foodstuff of all time. They possess curves that are voluptuous yet not obscene, and to eat a perfect, ripe, buttery one is in itself an experience matched only by orgasmic bliss. Well, perhaps that is pushing it a bit, but they do have a history of getting people ready for action as it were.

The Aztecs named the avocado 'ahuacatl', which roughly translates as 'lovely bollock', and in their culture it was such a symbol of fertility and rampant bonking that a village's brides-to-be were kept safely chaste and locked away during lovely bollock gathering season – which is quite understandable.

These days everyone is free to feel the curve of its dinosaur hide, the satisfying schlurp of the stone slipping out, and above all the smooth sensuality it adds to a host of dishes. Best of all, though, is avocado at its simplest – halved, stoned and served with a drizzle of vinaigrette.

Banana

They're sweet, creamy, gently curved and between 6 and 10 inches long. Do I have to spell it out? Perhaps because of this they have been used for centuries as a symbol of temptation and debauchery. Bananas are also an incredibly good source of vitamin B and slow-release energy – perfect for tennis matches and sexual triathlons – and are at their most incredible best if slit open, stuffed full of chocolate, wrapped in foil and oven-baked or barbecued.

Basil

Long regarded as a herb with special medicinal properties in Eastern civilisations, and revered throughout the Mediterranean, basil is an essential ingredient in a whole range of dishes. I can't claim that my research has revealed it to have any particular aphrodisiac effects, but it is damn tasty – in the subtle, hinting way that means you notice, desperately, its absence rather than its inclusion. The sweeter, oriental varieties are great for Thai cooking, and kept in a pot as a growing herb it adds a warm, clean aroma to rooms, making you think you're in Marrakesh, even if you're really in Margate.

Bay Leaves

With a gentle wafting dream of a flavour, one or two bay leaves added to a sauce and removed before serving can turn something bland and unexciting into a hintingly cheeky romantic dish.

Brazil Nuts

Brazil nuts are the chunkiest nuts there are. Aside from the gentle sway in their hips, they are thought to be a good source of selenium, which helps stimulate endorphin production and leaves us feeling healthy all round.

Cardamom

The seedpods have a deliciously warm and spicy flavour that works incredibly well with milk to leave you feeling happy and soothed, making cardamom a perfect pre-bed or breakfast ingredient. Indeed, Hindu recipe books have treasured this spice for centuries, suggesting that the ground pods, boiled in milk with a little honey, make a knockout impotence cure for men. There may be something in this, as randy scientists have identified cineole contained within the sexy little pods, and this stuff is known to stimulate the central nervous system.

Carrots

Although carrots contain a touch of myristic acid – the purportedly hallucinogenic and mood-altering component of nutmeg – they are no longer thought to possess any specific aphrodisiac qualities. In the past, carrots were feasted upon by Middle Eastern royalty, believing they provided stamina for those long Arabian nights spent pleasuring the harem, and, of course, good night vision is always an advantage.

Celery

It is chiefly the seeds of the humble and unassuming celery plant that have a history of use as an aphrodisiac. The Romans in particular were fond of celery, dedicating the plant to Pluto, who was their favourite god of sex. We now know that celery is packed full of vitamins A, B and C and stimulates the pituitary gland, which has the important responsibility in our body of releasing sex hormones.

Chilli

Chillies come in a wide and sometimes bewildering array of shapes, sizes and strengths. What they have in common is a dose of capsaicin, reputed to provide a euphoric, natural high, and a supply of vitamin C. Chilli – especially dried, such as the fearsome and erroneously named cayenne pepper (*capsicum annuum*) – also acts as a releaser of endorphins, from which their reputation as an aphrodisiac probably derives. Be warned though: put too many of these babies in a dish and you'll spend the evening crying and making camp and cartoonish faces at one another as you go steadily redder.

Milk and alcoholic drinks will take away some of the sting from over-chillied tongues and lips – water will do absolutely nothing, unless you are Wile E. Coyote, in which case it will make steam issue forth from your ears.

Chocolate

If you've not worked out that sex and chocolate are interlinked then you've been missing all the fun – as well as all the not-so-subtle hints the advertisers have been dropping since you were little. Oral sex anyone? No, just a flake is it? Anyway, there seems to be some scientific basis to chocolate's reputation as a wicked aphrodisiac. Firstly, it is packed with caffeine which, as coffee and cola drinkers will know, helps to shuffle you forward from the back of the sleepy shelf, right to the precipice of mental alertness. But that's not all: chocolate is also rich in phenylethylamine. That's easy for *you* to say, you think. Phenywotsit – which we'll call PEA – is best described as a natural amphetamine and antidepressant, and is produced within our own bodies when we are in love. Hence chocolate can be warming, soothing and, yes, sexually arousing.

Now, some of the reputation chocolate has may, scientifically speaking, be a load of old cobblers reiterated *ad infititum* by the advertising community, but its position as a comfort food, in rituals of courtship, and especially as a sauce to be licked and nibbled from everywhere imaginable, makes chocolate a rude food like no other.

Cloves
The Chinese, who purportedly first used cloves in cooking, and the Romans both believed in the curative and aphrodisiac powers of cloves. Today cloves are used principally in desserts, where they make us feel warm, happy and slightly fruity.

Coco-de-Mer
I've never tasted one so have no recipes for the giant nut of the palm *Codociea maldivica*, but it deserves a mention as it holds the coveted honour of being the world's largest fruit, and it is also quite simply the world's rudest. This massive nut, which can weigh in at anywhere up to 20 kg, resembles a woman's lower torso in exquisite anatomical detail. Furthermore, the nut's jelly-like flesh is famed locally for its powerful aphrodisiac properties. Ladies and gentlemen, we have a contender for the rudest food ever.

Unfortunately, coco-de-mer nuts are not generally available in your local supermarket, unless you live in the Seychelles.

Coffee
Brewed from the roasted beans of *Rubiaceae coffea*, the drink we know as coffee can be both a soothing comfort and a

jolting and invigorating kick-start. It is thought to increase blood flow, heart rate and mental alertness – all of which also occur when we are sexually aroused. A nice coffee after a meal is delightful, but it does not necessarily need to be caffeinated as the ritual is often enough. Indeed, my heartfelt advice is to drink coffee in moderation, not just because a reliance upon it will ultimately cause you stress and will become unhealthy, but because after two double espressos even the owner of the steadiest hands imaginable will become a jittery bag of fidgets.

Coriander

This herb has been used throughout history as an aphrodisiac, but my own experiments were scuppered by my abundant overuse of it. There are only a few dishes that aren't enlivened by a handful of fresh, chopped coriander, and it is especially sexy in hot and spicy Indian and Thai dishes, giving them a cool yet tangy air of sexy sophistication.

Cream

An incredibly sexy food to cook with because it has a smooth and slinky version of the Midas touch, turning all it touches to velvet. However, it truly comes into its own when it is taken out of the kitchen and into the bedroom, maybe with some strawberries, maybe as ice cream, and licked from every smooth and wrinkled surface you can find. Especially fun and manageable whipped, and an evening spent with your partner and a can of the UHT stuff could be one of the best evenings of your life …

Eggs

It is difficult to find a more obvious symbol of sex. While eggs provide a source of protein and help contribute to a healthy, balanced diet, there is not really any compelling evidence that they are, in themselves, aphrodisiacs. However, including them in a romantic meal may add to the poignancy of the moment – proving to you both that life is a cycle, that sex is natural, sex is good, that not everybody does it, but everybody should. Now I feel a song coming on – look what you've made me do.

Escargot

Snails. Perhaps, while they are alive, it can be argued that these are not the sexiest of creatures – indeed, many people harbour a fear of the undulating, slimy, home-carrying snail quite out of proportion to any real threat it poses, and being captured by a speedy, house-sized, carnivorous and hungry snail is a common childhood nightmare. Or was that just me?

Nonetheless, snails are famous as an aphrodisiac delicacy, and are often served with garlic butter so powerful that most concerns about taste and texture are simply blown away.

Fennel

A massive body of scientific research suggests that – along with pumpkin – the aroma of liquorice (and liquorice aroma-ed things) is one of the most effective food turn-ons for both men and women. Certainly a claim worth investigating, and even if untrue you'll have lost nothing, as the slightly ovoid and peculiarly hand-shaped fennel bulb makes a delicious addition to creamy soups, while the seed works well with fish.

Fig

While the fig is a strangely unforgettable fruit, it hardly seems to exude instantly sexy charisma. However, closer examination reveals the skin to have a throbbing hue, as if something fearsomely rampant has been locked away inside and is looking for day release. Gently slice one open and you'll see what all the fuss is about – a beautifully moist, red-pink flesh radiates out from a central orifice exuding the sweetest aroma ever. Figs were Cleopatra's favourite fruit: say no more.

Garlic

Garlic gets a lot of bad press. Despite its evil- and vampire-warding qualities, there is often a tendency to hang negative connotations on garlic's distinct and pungent aroma. This has not always been so: cultures around the world and throughout history, from the ancient Egyptians to the Japanese, have employed garlic as an aphrodisiac, as well as using it for its curative properties.

There is little doubt today that garlic is a kitchen essential, and a rude food cook without some would be no kind of rude food cook at all, for it provides a certain special kick and oomph to the simplest of dishes. My personal trials — which I can hardly claim to have conducted with scientific rigour — have demonstrated that garlic enlivens the senses and makes you feel that little bit more alive. And, yeah, it smells: just make sure your partner has some, too.

Ginger

This curiously gnarled root has been used for centuries as an aphrodisiac throughout the Indian subcontinent and Asia, and is widely recommended by herbalists today as a cure for impotence. Despite its appeal as an essential ingredient in Chinese and South-East Asian cooking, it is worth noting that its sexual association is not peculiar to the Orient. The practice of baking gingerbread men originated in Europe as part of a ritual aimed at landing eligible maidens a suitable husband.

Hazel and Hazelnut

Hazel has strong associations with pre-Christian pagan rituals. At May Day time, the festival historically known as Beltain, the women of the villages had their private parts twanged, stroked and thwacked with hazel rods in the hope that some of the fertility god Donar's prolific sexual prowess would, er, rub off on them. Meanwhile, hazelnuts were used as a representation of the phallus in rituals. It is not surprising that ancient aphrodisiac recipes for potions and so forth relied heavily on the roasted nuts or the oil derived from them. Hazel is still a symbol of fertility, as the hazel bush is one of the first to come into flower in the spring, and science tells us that hazelnuts are rich in vitamin E, which is associated with normal sexual function. They are also a tasty nibble.

Hemp

Far be it from me to condone or endorse the use of illegal substances in cooking – and one should be aware that the possession and sale of cannabis and its derivatives remain against the law, unless you're reading this in the Netherlands – but I'm reliably informed that a sparing sprinkle of cannabis leaf (specifically the dried flowering buds of the female plant) used in your favourite dish and, especially, in baking, heightens one's receptivity to taste and erogenous pleasure, and gives cornflakes a whole new lease of life. Similar chemical components are found in eucalyptus leaf, which may explain the koala's permanently strung out attitude towards life.

Honey

Honey, ba-ba-ba ba ba baaa, sugar sugar ... Where would we be without this stuff? Try and imagine if you'd never tasted it – no, if it had never existed at all. Aside from bees turning into little more than a mild annoyance during the summer months, some of the fun would drop away from the earth. Honey symbolises lightness, sweetness and sticky, messy love, and has done since humankind first discovered it. It features in the *Karma Sutra*, has been recommended as an aid to sexual health by everyone from the Ancient Greeks through to modern-day Hindus, and, of course, tradition states that newlyweds should seclude themselves after their wedding day, freed temporarily from the shackles of society, drink honey potions and make long, lingering love until the next new moon, a tradition we still practice today when we take honeymoons. So, if your spouse-to-be insists you settle for a weekend in Bognor, at least make sure you take a jar of the runny stuff along.

Ice

If you've never taken your lover to bed armed with little more than a box of ice cubes then I suggest you stop reading this book right now and get to it. But I won't tell you what to do with them — that would spoil the fun.

Mango

While mangoes have an incredibly vibrant colour and a unique, fibrous flesh, the sexiest thing about them is actually eating them. A truly ripe mango eaten in the correct manner (with the skin slit lengthways from top to tip, quartering the fruit, the flaps peeled away one by one, and the flesh juicily devoured) provides a slurping, sticky spectacle with many opportunities for lingering looks and naughty finger sucking.

Mushroom

In all their many forms, mushrooms provide compelling evidence for the existence of a super-intelligent Supreme Creator with a tragically puerile sense of humour. They are unquestionably the most phallic food ever. If an architect drew up plans for the erection (sorry) of a building that looked like a mushroom, protestors would flock to the construction site to, er, protest — yet God has got away with it all this time.

Mustard

This wickedly spicy crop turns up in bestseller The Bible, which claims it to be 'the greatest among herbs'. A possible reason for this is that at the time the New Testament first went to press, rubbing mustard on one's penis was a popular cure for a whole range of sexual deficiencies. I can only assume there is some science involved in this practice – the mustard may increase blood flow and open capillaries, for instance – but I wouldn't wholly advise it as it must be fairly painful. Instead, use mustard for the purpose nature surely intended – a dollop of the good English stuff for wonderful sausages, grainy French for perfect beef, and smooth Dijon for just about anything, but especially creamy mash and velvety salad dressings.

Nine-and-a-Half Weeks

The good bit sees the lead couple in a teasing food and sex orgy. Otherwise a reasonably disturbing tale of submission and control, the film is erotic in the sense that seeing Kim Basinger forced into depraved acts is erotic. Which I suppose it is. It has now become synonymous with food foreplay, paving the way for thousands of couples to don blindfolds and feed each other everything from chillies to strawberries – with the blindfoldees presumably imagining they are being fed by Kim herself or Mickey Rourke.

Nutmeg

As well as providing a formative drug experience for many a teenager, nutmeg is an extremely versatile ingredient. It can be used to spice up just about anything, and its warm, round and yet lingeringly tangy flavour is unique, powerful and heartening. It also contains myristic acid, a chemical found in the peyote cactus (as well as parsley and carrots; vegetables which, to my knowledge, no one has ever tried to snort), and this could be the reason for its reputation as a potent aphrodisiac.

If you love nutmeg – and it is an easy nut to fall for – my advice is to invest in one of those little graters with a small container at the top for holding the nut. The other advice I would offer is to remember that not everyone will share your passion: use nutmeg only sparingly (no more than a pinch or two in any dish), as it can easily overwhelm all other flavours.

It goes without saying that snorting lines of ground nutmeg is foolhardy, inadvisable and unlikely to impress your present partner or a potential beau. It is neither big nor clever: it's dangerous.

Onion

As the Roman author Martial said in AD something or other, 'If your wife is old and your member exhausted, eat onions aplenty', although he was never too clear as to whether this would give the said organ fresh wood, as it were, or merely put off the old other half's amorous advances. Onions are, however, mentioned extensively in ancient Arabic and Hindu love manuals; it is traditional for French newlyweds to be served onion soup on the morning after their wedding (to revive those flagging libidos, presumably); and there is evidence that ancient Egypt's high priests were banned from going anywhere near these pungent, multi-layered balls ... so make of that what you will.

Oyster

The three things people most commonly associate with oysters is that 1) they taste horrible, 2) they are fearsomely potent aphrodisiacs, and 3) that Casanova ate bucketloads of them each morning in the bath, and all three of these statements could be true in their own ways. Oysters certainly have a unique taste, and not everyone will like them. They taste, essentially, of the sea in a fresh, briny sort of way, and swallowing them whole will not change this fact or make it easy to ignore. So, if they're not your bag, they're not your bag.

Their power as an aphrodisiac, meanwhile, will really depend on who you're with when you eat them, remembering that love is possibly the best aphrodisiac – although it may run a close second behind sheer unbridled lust. Oysters are low in fat, high in protein and are an excellent source of zinc, which helps produce testosterone and of which a supply in the body is vital for normal sexual functioning. International opinion is largely agreed that they do the trick. As for the highly-sexed Casanova – well, he can't have done that *every* morning, can he?

Parsley

Gone are the days when that little sprig of parsley was left on the side of the plate, wondered at by all inexperienced diners. Should I eat it? And if not, why is it there in the first place? For a rude food meal – especially one that looks like it might lead somewhere else – the parsley should really be eaten, as it has the effect of sweetening up your secretions be you a man or a woman. This could be especially helpful if you've just eaten a load of asparagus or garlic, foods with a reputation for making your bodily juices smell.

Pepper

Black, ground and crushed; green and whole; white, light and fragrant – pepper is to rude food cookery what gold is to Fort Knox. Invest in a good grinder – it *will* be worth it.

I don't think there's any need to go as far as the ancient Arabic penis expansion recipe, which suggests grinding it up with lavender, honey and ginger and rubbing the stuff all over the, ahem, longitudinally challenged member in question.

Pine Nuts

The kernels from pinecones were waxed lyrical by the poet Ovid and were prescribed by Ancient Greek doctors to treat impotence. They have been putting the warm, nutty kick in pesto for centuries.

Quince

Forget passion fruit and pomegranates – quince is the fruit with the sexiest history. Dedicated to Aphrodite by the ancient Greeks, and to Venus by the Romans, quince is one of the oldest known fruits, having been grown throughout the Mediterranean since 300 BC at least, and there is some evidence to suggest that the apple mentioned in the Bible is none other than the saucy quince pear.

Quince is traditionally eaten at weddings, perhaps because the seeds and the mucilage (or sticky) cells of the pear are thought to make it a potent aphrodisiac.

Rice

An Eastern symbol of fertility, and one of the world's oldest cultivated crops, rice is far from a mere staple. It is thrown at weddings to bless the couple with a happy and fruitful relationship, and in Japan and China, eating rice from the same bowl as your beau is used to signify engagement, while rice wine (sake) is a key component in Japanese marriage ceremonies.

Rose

Roses are symbolic of all we know to be good and uncomplicated in romance, yet at the same time they are intricately complex, delicate flowers. Fortunately they're not just for show. The soft, inner petals can be washed and sprinkled into salads to add a gentle yet lingering fragrance.

Rude Food

The present volume you're reading is not the first *Rude Food*: a book using the same name appeared in 1983 and was to revolutionise coffee tables across the world with its soft-focus shots of nudes seductively licking butter from rounded asparagus tips, dribbling cream over nipples and bellies, and balancing spinach in unlikely places. Hugely entertaining and erotic in the way that soft porn from the eighties generally isn't.

Anyone planning a *Nine-and-half Weeks*-style romp may want

to get their hands on a copy for a bit of forward planning, and as it fetches a pretty good second-hand price you'll be able to sell it to pay for the damage you did to the hotel sheets.

Saffron

Weight for weight, saffron is one of the most expensive substances in the world. It is made from the stigma hairs of a small crocus: as each crocus has three stigma hairs, and 1 oz of saffron requires something in the region of 15,000 hand-picked hairs, the cost is hardly surprising. Its reputation as an aphrodisiac is, however, without parallel: it is quoted as a vital sex aid in Arabic, Hindu, Roman and Greek love manuals, and its warm red glow gives some dishes the little boost they need.

Spanish Fly

A strong contender for 'most potent aphrodisiac ever', Spanish fly is something you certainly won't see in your local supermarket, unless you are reading this in Roman times, when apparently the stuff was used in abundance. The extract from the crushed shells of *Lytta vesicatoria* – a large emerald-green creature, very unlike a fly, called the blister beetle – was purportedly used by the Empress Livia to work her family members into orgiastic bliss for which she could later blackmail them (although one would imagine they were all at it anyway, having seen *Up Pompeii*). Nearly two thousand years later, the Marquis de Sade fed Spanish-fly-laced sweets to prostitutes in an effort to scientifically gauge its effect and have a giggle at the same time.

Although many of the stories that have propelled Spanish fly to its mythical status may well not be true at all, it is known that its active ingredient, cantharidine, causes an increased flow of blood to the groin (as cantharidine irritates the urethra), resulting in arousal in both men and women and often, in men, a permanent erection.

Unfortunately, this permanent stiffy-thing, known as Priapism (after Priapus, a magnificently-endowed Greek god, although 'permanent stiffy-thing' is the technical term), is generally agreed to be painful rather than erotic, and is probably the least of your worries when dealing with Spanish fly. Other documented side effects of cantharidine are mental illness and, disturbingly, death. The Marquis de Sade's prostitutes, for instance, became horribly ill and the misguided venture saw the Marquis on the stand for poisoning. So kids: Just Say No.

Spinach

This, of course, is the stuff that Popeye made famous, and countless millions of children have grown up wondering why, when they eat it, they don't get the same bulging forearms as the pug-ugly creation of the Spinach Marketing Board (probably). Spinach is, as we all know, a good source of vitamins and iron, but that's no reason to go eating the tinned stuff, which is invariably disgusting. Fresh spinach makes for light and fun eating, is superb in salads and, when steamed and reduced a little, can be stuffed into all sorts of unlikely places.

Beware, though, of the classic First Date Pitfall: stay well clear of the stuff or bring a good sturdy toothpick because, as Murphy's Law states, if it can get stuck between your teeth, it will.

Strawberry

Strawberries are the most sensual of the summer fruits. Sweet and juicy, strawberries are not only delicious but also good for you, being packed with vitamin C and having very few calories. Of course, they are also erotically nipple-like: especially when they're covered in sugar and cream and pushed between your lover's lips. To add flavour to the cream, add a drop of vanilla essence and a sprinkling of icing sugar before whipping it.

Strawberry season is early summer, so pack a hamper with the one you love and pick your own. If you come across the tiny, wild variety (*Fragaria vesca*), have a good, long nibble on those, too.

Sweet Potato

Sweet potatoes are incredibly tasty. Underneath the face they present to the world – that rough, gnarled and grotty skin – there lurks a lurid flesh that is a delight to reveal, boil and mash. As a comfort food I think they beat their tuber relative, the potato, and are much prettier. Sweet potatoes, and their cousins yams, turn out to be brimming with a chemical called diosgenin, which mimics the effect of female sex hormones, and hence is used in all sorts of aphrodisiac potions.

Toad

Like the emerald-green blister beetle (see Spanish fly), the humble toad lived out a peaceful existence until humans realised that their dead flayed bodies were of far more use than their croaky mating calls. These toads are the source of a traditional Chinese medicine called Chan Su, which is used as a local anaesthetic on the skin – and one should note here that this is often a good sign that one shouldn't be eating the stuff. And, perhaps predictably, Chan Su has been the cause of numerous deaths when taken internally. Although I'm not speaking from personal experience, I wouldn't imagine this was one to hunt down with vigour. Try Toad-in-the-Hole instead: much nicer.

Tomatoes

You say tomayto, and may well have tomarto hurled back in response, but the Italians prefer to consummate their long-running affair with the tomato by giving it a sexy name: *pomodoro*, or love apple. However, it should be remembered that the Italians, with their staple of pasta and sauce, were not always the tomato's friend: the barmy Romans tried to ban the tomato because they thought it was poisonous. Enjoying a slightly better press these days, the tomato is certainly a sexy fruit (although it tends to masquerade as a vegetable in supermarkets), and since it is red — the colour of passion and the colour of love — it is an essential addition to your forays into rude cookery.

It is a statistical truth that 79 per cent of the population have had a tin of economy peeled plum tomatoes in the back of one of their cupboards for over a year. Isn't it about time you got yours out?

Truffles

The truffle seems an unlikely choice as a symbol of wealth, power, indulgence and decadence, as it is small, crinkled and dark, rather like a brain exposed to too much *Family Fortunes*. It is certainly not a sexy object in itself, and although there is a certain teasing androgyny about the apparent lack of a food category in which to place it, it is in fact a sort of tuber. This places it roughly in the potato family, and on top of this slight, truffles are usually located by using trained pigs that were, only minutes before, snuffling around eating each other's poo.

Against these culinary black marks is the incredibly dense, rich flavour the truffles provide when grated into any dish (but especially eggs and omelettes, cream and pasta sauces) and the warm nutty feeling of wellbeing truffle in a meal provides. Truffles are the kind of thing you might buy on holiday, thinking it to be A Good Idea At The Time. It's worth knowing what to do with them, because they do taste delicious. Alternatively, you can buy bottles of truffle oil, usually olive oil infused with the taste of the little blighters — this stuff makes a delicious accompaniment to shellfish dishes.

Unagi

In Britain this is better known as a pie-filler, or is served up in a rich, thick jelly, for unagi is the Japanese name for the humble eel. Visually, eels are, of course, rather phallic, but they are also reasonably unsexy creatures leading grim and brutal lives, and lack the aesthetic quality an animal must have for someone to think, 'Mmm. That looks tasty – lemmeeatitnow.' However, in Japan, eel flesh is both expensive and revered as it is said to have powerful aphrodisiac properties. It is also very, very tasty, making for brilliant sushi. If you ever go to Japan, have a bowl of rice topped with it. Or, if you ever go to that Japanese place round the corner … I promise you'll never look at jellied eels in the same light again.

Vanilla

I read somewhere that vanilla pods are such a good aphrodisiac that they were named after the female sex organs (with the Spanish word for vagina being markedly similar). I'm not sure as to what extent this is bunkum, but there could be something in it. Vanilla is remarkably pleasant to smell and it is inhaling its delicious aroma that has a mood-changing effect, rather than vanilla being an aphrodisiac food *per se*.

Walnut

Poor Jupiter must have received quite a ribbing from his fellow gods, for these gnarled, wrinkled nuts are named after his testicles – hence the Latin name (*Juglans regia*) that slyly refers to Jupiter's Balls. The Roman tradition of throwing these at wedding ceremonies (where rice would usually be thrown) still persists to this day, while saucy minx Cleopatra ate sphinx-sized portions of them, believing they would increase her libido. As if she needed any help!

Xanat, Ylang Ylang, Zinc

However fascinating as Xanat and Zinc may be, I'd like to dedicate this space to all of those who've aided and abetted the creation of this book. With all my love and deepest thanks to …

Sheila Cox - Expert Mother, Toad Holer and Choc Mousser
Summerly DeVito - Italian Correspondent and Oyster-Swallowing Expert
Sanchia Lovell - Picnic Reporter
Tomu, Debido and Mizuho - Japanese Senpai
Rachael Osborne - Strawberry Consultant & Editor Extraordinaire
Hannah Lewis – Chief Vodka Taster
Brian O'Faolin - Iberian Researcher
Steve Willis – Ladies' Fashion Guru
Hannah Hill – Bed Catering Consultant

As ever, to all at Westbourne Villas for your love and kindness, and to everyone who replied to the Internet questionnaire (and whose identities I've sworn to protect …).

LUKE COX xxx

The BBQ & Campfire Recipe Book

by Luke Cox

£4.99 • paperback • 1 84024 244 2 • 129 x 198 mm/160 pp

Incinerated sausages and cremated marshmallows? Not with this book!

If you're yearning for something delicious and different to get your teeth into this summer, then this is the book for you. *The BBQ & Campfire Recipe Book* is packed with recipes, from Old Favourites and quick-and-easys to something more adventurous to impress your friends. Practical, full of useful hints and BBQ insider knowledge, this is the indispensable companion to the Great Outdoors.

Picnic Food

by Sanchia Lovell

£4.99 • paperback • 1 84024 365 1 • 129 x 198 mm/160 pp

Great food for the great outdoors.

Everyone enjoys a picnic, and this book proves how diverse meals alfresco can be. From delightfully messy children's parties to beach barbies, romantic riverbank lunches and the ultimate sandwich, this book is the definitive guide to the outdoor eating experience.

Liberally scattered with advice and cheeky suggestions from literary greats Shakespeare, Hardy, Moley and Ratty.

For a current catalogue and a full listing of
Summersdale books, visit our website:

www.summersdale.com